WHAT

IS STANDING IN THE

WAY

THE JOURNEY OF BECOMING YOUR BEST SELF

ANDRE J. WICKS

ISBN: 979-8-7299018-8-3

Copy editing by: David Kilmer
Cover design by: Xavier Wicks and Andre J. Wicks
Author photo by: Xavier Wicks

To my family, thank you. Specifically, to Michelle, Isaac, Xavier, Olivia, and Pearl. Your love and support are a fountain of encouragement to me. Also, to my family, all the family, friends, and mentors that love me, support me, and who are committed to helping me become my best self. It is the only way I am able to help others become their best self.

Contents

Preface

In August of 2019 I travelled outside of Chicago, Illinois. I was speaking to the Elgin U46 School District during their return to school professional development days. It was a two-day event; I had all middle school and high school staff on the first day and all elementary staff the second day. At this training I was leading a session I had taken hundreds of people through before. It was titled **What is standing in the way?**

This was one of my bread-and-butter sessions. In it I shared a story about an acquaintance I knew growing up. On the first day, with the middle school and high school staff, I told the story of my acquaintance, as best I could through his eyes. I dropped clues along the way that got the audience wondering, who *is* this acquaintance? In my story my acquaintance struggled getting out of his own way. It was as though he was repetitively losing games of tug-o-war. He would get overpowered by the foe on the other end of the rope time after time. He was not losing gracefully either, it was more like the tripping over his feet and falling flat on his face kind of losing.

By the end of the acquaintance story, the introduction to the session, I revealed the truth. The truth surprised some staff and confirmed a hunch for others that, yes, the acquaintance I knew growing up was actually me.

"Why did you describe yourself as an acquaintance?" someone in the audience called out.

I asked, "Why do you think?" The audience member said she thought it was for two reasons. First, for dramatic effect. Which worked, she said. Secondly, she said it could be because you really were an acquaintance to yourself then. You *really* didn't *know* who you were.

I said, "First, ma'am, you are spot on. Secondly, thank you. To be honest, when I prepared this session several months ago, describing myself as an acquaintance was absolutely for dramatic effect. But what you have just picked up on, within 30 minutes of hearing my story, is profound. Even for me."

How many of you are walking through life, right now, feeling like you are repetitively losing games of tug-o-war? Not only are you in a losing game of tug-o-war, but you can't figure out why you are always in this tug-o-war to begin with. And, on top of that, are you scratching your head because you think you may recognize the foe at the other end of the rope?

As I walked among the staff during a breakout, I came upon a woman who was moved by my story. When I approached her, she gave me a big smile and asked me if I had a book. At the time, I let her know I did not have a book.

She looked me straight in the eyes, and said with a degree of purpose that is indescribable, "Well, child, YOU need to write a book!" Her conviction that I should write a book was the nudge I needed. The reason why this nudge was different, the reason why it had the ultimate affect of me following through with the writing, was the fact that she genuinely believed that my book would help people.

I believe she was right.

I believe it will too.

Part I: *What* is standing in the way?

Chapter 1

The problem is YOU

"If there is no enemy within,
the enemy outside can do us no harm." –African Proverb

Every good story has a villain, an adversary who stands in the hero's way and threatens to destroy all that is good.

This story has such a character, too.

But unlike a classic crime thriller with all its twists and turns, I am going to give you the big reveal right up front.

First of all, you are the hero of this story. You, like me, like most of us, are on a quest for good things. You seek health, wealth, happiness, peace, joy, love, intelligence, wisdom, and patience. And yet these things can be quite difficult to find. Sometimes it feels like barriers continue to be thrown up, one after the other. We can't climb those hurdles to be our best selves, let alone to help anyone else.

Yes, it's true, there is an evil genius trying to thwart you, throwing up all those barriers and no doubt even chuckling with glee like a cartoon supervillain. But that crazy, evil genius of this story, that annoying, even frightening character who is absolutely bound and determined to derail your dreams? That adversary is closer than you think.

There's really no other way to break this to you:

The problem is you.

And what is standing in your way?

The answer, again, is you.

Yes, you are the hero of your story, but you are also (occasionally, often, or always) the villain.

And now that you know the big twist, you can put the book down and walk away. Or, if you're like me, you might be interested to know a little more about this fascinating villain.

What drives their dastardly deeds? Can they ever be stopped? What are their superpowers? Their weaknesses?

And if the hero finally overcomes the villain, what happens next?

Well, my friends, we are about to find out.

You may not be surprised or offended to find the true source of your pain and problems. Or you may be very surprised, and maybe a little offended. It doesn't matter. The problem is still you.

I know this with certainty, because for years, my problem was me.

As a younger man, I found myself stuck in my career, and in life. I had been angry. I had been utterly discontented. I was bitter about the hurdles in life and always looking for a bad guy.

Then one day I finally found my villain. It was a moment just as dramatic as any superhero showdown. There he was, in all his glory, glaring back at me from my bathroom mirror.

My villain was me.

That moment, the sudden realization that I was my own biggest problem, changed my life forever. It was the first step on the journey of becoming my best self.

Does it seem hard to believe? I can assure you it's true. That thing holding you back from everything you've ever wanted, for the last few months, years, or maybe decades... is yourself.

How I wish I would have figured this out years ago. But such is life, right? It is only in reflecting backwards that we gain the greatest value forwards, and oftentimes from the toughest of experiences.

That has been the story of my life, a story I'd like to share with you. Getting out of my own way made a radical difference in my life, my relationships, and my work. Today, I am on a path of continuous improvement. I anticipate the potential for learning and inspiration in every single interaction. I am a man transformed, so I, in turn, can be transformational.

Today I live my life inspired, and I live my life motivated. In this book, I will share what works for me, and encourage you to begin your own journey of overcoming yourself. Together, we are going to find ways to live with intention and integrity. We are going to experience life to the fullest and help others do the same.

Getting out of your own way, and then staying out of your way, takes repetition. It's like learning a new sport; in this case, the most important sport of your life. This practice is not easy, but it will absolutely transform you, I promise.

The life-changing knowledge I will share comes from high achievers, from children, from philosophers. You will begin by putting their ideas into practice. Then, for the rest of your life, you will continue to seek to learn, listen, watch, read and experience things that continue to make you your very best self. When you build a foundation like this, over time it will continue to become ever stronger and more unshakeable.

Let's start with the African proverb: *If there is no enemy within, the enemy outside can do us no harm.*

No other person, situation, shortcoming, or adversary is as powerful as you. As you reflect on your life, you will see it is so. That time your team lost? That failure to achieve? That missed opportunity? That enemy was you.

What kept you from enrolling in that master's degree program? From writing that book? From training for and running that half marathon? Look closer at that foe who has kept you from losing weight, from seeking the help you need for depression, from advocating for yourself, or from kicking a habit that is taking years off your life. Think about the very best and most successful people, groups, teams, organizations, systems, and businesses. Their inner foe is no longer standing in their way. And that makes them nearly undefeatable.

I have listened to a lot of Eric Thomas, who is one of the most sought-after motivational speakers on the planet. He has his own brand and has a PhD. He has authored multiple books, has nearly one million YouTube subscribers and more than nine hundred YouTube videos. He has a wonderful wife and kids and is the first man in his family to actually raise his own children. Eric has beat the odds. He likes to say, "You are where you are because of who you are." Before he worked with the NFL and the NBA, before he had earned his PhD, before he was a world-renowned author and public speaker, Eric was homeless. He came from a long line of men who had abandoned their families. When he was still a teenager, his own mother kicked him out of the house. He ate out of garbage cans, slept in vacant buildings, and believed his life was hopeless.

Today, Eric will tell you this: The key to changing *everything* in his life was changing just *one thing*. And that one thing was himself. If you've heard him speak, you know Eric tells a moving story. If you haven't, set this book down, search YouTube for "Eric Thomas, How bad do you want it?" and see and hear for yourself! "I had to stop making excuses," he says. "I wasn't gonna get another daddy. I wasn't gonna get another momma. If I wanted my circumstances to change, I needed to change."

He's right. If you are not *where* you want to be, you are not *who* you need to be. It is entirely up to you. What a wise truth.

How many successful people have *eased* their way to the top of the mountain? How many successful marriages just sort of *happened*? How many school leaders raised graduation rates by accepting the status quo and just *getting by*? None. Growth and improvement only happen in the midst of the struggle.

It's natural to look for the easy way in, or the easy way out. All of us have done it before. But I want to challenge you to *seek* a challenge instead.

I remember a point, early in my professional career, that I looked for the easy way. I had been a classroom teacher and a head coach, and I was successful at both.

It seemed natural that the next step was school leadership. I completed my coursework and internship in preparation. I thought I was ready. And I was confident I had an inside track. One of the kids I had taught and coached was the son of the school director. She played a heavy hand in hiring school administrators.

In retrospection, I was looking for the easy way. There I was, with no more than three months in training as an intern, and I thought I could leverage a relationship to get my way in.

That relationship did get me an interview. And that's all.

I did not get the job.

I was stunned, offended and angry. I remained bitter for months. *Clearly,* I fumed to myself and anyone within earshot, *I interviewed brilliantly. How did they miss the best candidate for the job?*

So, I blamed the system. I blamed the school director and, absurdly, I even blamed the interview questions. What a fool I was.

People around me gave me some very wise advice, which I initially ignored in my stupor. They told me maybe I wasn't ready for leadership. Perhaps, despite my inflated opinion of my own performance, I *had* interviewed poorly. And they were right.

Even worse, because of my unpleasant attitude and complaining in the months following my failed interview, I did even more damage. It's quite likely I cost myself other shots at school leadership thereafter.

But during this uncomfortable time, I finally confronted the truth of the matter. The problem all along had been me.

The problem was *still* me!

That's when I looked in the mirror. I saw I would have to become comfortable being uncomfortable. I would have to be vulnerable and transparent about my weaknesses. I would need to confront them directly and make a commitment to turn them into strengths. I needed to get the heck out of my own way and turn my best self loose. So that is what I set out to do. I decided to make it my life's work. And that work continues to this day, to this hour, to this moment. That work never ends.

As bestselling author and lecturer Joe Dispenza says, "Your personality creates your personal reality."

Put another way, *if you want to change your personal reality, you have to change your personality.*

I certainly had to change mine. As a child and then as a young man, both my personality and my reality were defined by anger. That anger might have come from any number of factors: Abuse, neglect, poverty, hunger and the violence in our home, to name a few. I'm certain the trauma I experienced as a child, and the environment I was raised in, played a huge role in my anger. For others, it might bring about a personality of depression, manipulation, obsession, cowardice, spite, addiction, or an unhealthy combination of these things.

My anger got the best of me so many times. It brought out the worst in me and in those around me. When I was angry, I didn't add value to the world; I diminished it. And I was angry all the time.

My anger affected friendships and relationships. My anger intimidated people. My anger masked the fact that I had much more potential than most people gave me credit for. In all these ways, my anger defined my personality and shaped my world.

Sometimes my friends would exploit my anger. They knew I would do mean things to other people when provoked, and so they would provoke me. My anger in these unfortunate moments gave me a bad reputation.

And then, one day, I saw the fear in someone's eyes because of me.

As a high school track coach, I was very proud of the opportunities and challenges of creating an environment for young men to develop into men with integrity. But early in my coaching career my priorities were mixed up. I allowed my past to shape a personality, and that personality in turn created a less-than-desirable reality. While I certainly wanted to help young men succeed, I also felt a burning need to succeed. Problem was, my search for success as a coach was fuelled by my pride. That pride came from assuming I had to prove to the world, or at least those who followed track and field, that I was a force to be reckoned with. Looking back, I can see how my need to prove something most likely had to do with a complex I had developed throughout childhood from neglect and disapproval.

To win track meets you must have athletes. Putting people in the right events on the right day matters, too. But really, you need to start with solid athletes. And I had them. At the same time, they were also high school kids. And so, they did what high school kids do. They made mistakes. As teachers and coaches, we have a role to play when those mistakes are made. We need to serve as an example. We are supposed to care for those student athletes, to support them and guide them. And occasionally I failed in that role.

One April afternoon in 2006, I came out to address the team for our usual pre-practice meeting. Yet this wasn't going to be a typical meeting. I had an agenda. I was determined to teach these kids, once and for all, how to man up and take care of their responsibilities. As the boys piled into the stands at Hart Field, I wasted no time. Their chatter and laughter turned to silence as I lit into them. And I mean an instant combustion that blew up like a wildfire. I was so fired up that the fire from my inner dragon must have scorched the eyebrows of my star sprinter who happened to be sitting right in front of me.

Grades. That was the cause of my anger; an anger that manifested itself, not in caring, supportive, or guiding feedback, but in me screaming at those boys. I furrowed my brow. I waved my arms and breathed fire. Unfortunately, and uncharacteristically, I cursed. And after all that yelling, I kicked all the athletes and coaches out of practice. I sent them all home with an angry, foul-mouthed ultimatum: get it together or you're done.

Over grades? Yeah, now it seems pathetic on my part. The thing was, it was selfish. My primary motivation, if I was being honest with myself, was I wanted them to bring their grades up so we could win contests. As I stormed past one of my athletes on my way back into the locker room, he quickly stepped to avoid me. As I looked up and into his eyes, I saw it. It was not admiration for the wonderful example of a man he wanted to emulate. It was fear.

I went back to the coaches' office and sat, all by myself. I had no one to reflect with. No one to tell me how foolish I had just been. I had kicked everyone out. Pushed everyone away. So, I had to sit with what I had just done, alone.

That was a low point for me. That look of fear struck me to the core. I knew I could be an angry person, but I never saw myself as threatening. Seeing that fear was a watershed moment. It made me recognize that my personality was playing a major role in my personal reality. Although it took many years of work, along with counseling and the love of others to help me, I resolved not to cause that kind of fear in someone ever again. Later in the book I will tell you how; how the choice to love others has allowed me to avoid such a pitfall.

Have you ever experienced analysis paralysis? Most of the time we are paralyzed by the fear of what *might* happen instead of being propelled by the confidence of what we know *can* happen. Our thoughts become our worst enemy, when instead they could be our greatest ally. It is human nature to assume the worst. And if we have experienced hardship or trauma, it becomes even easier to fear instead of to hope.

Isn't it diabolical the tricks our inner villain can play? Even when the most likely, most desirable outcome is staring us in the face, we continue to focus only on the unlikely, unhappy outcome. If you're like me, you realize with anger that you missed another opportunity. You vow never to doubt yourself again. Then you do it all over again.

Why? Because you are conditioned to think a certain way. And that thinking will continue to produce the same undesirable results. The only way to change your conditioning is through daily intentionality. Taking control of your thoughts takes regular exercise, in much the same way we exercise a muscle to make it stronger. That exercise lies in choosing things that change the present, which will soon become the past. In this way, you rewire those unhelpful short-circuits in your brain. You change your personality, and that changes your reality forever.

There you go. A glimpse inside your head, where both the hero and the villain reside. The obstacles, of how we think and how we behave, that have stood between you and everything you've ever dreamed of. The wall of you.

Now the cat is out of the bag. The secret is revealed.

And now that you know the good guys and bad guys, the real question remains.

How are you going to write your own story? Who will triumph, the hero or the villain?

Now that you know it is you who is standing in the way of exactly what you want to achieve most with your life, which direction are you going to go? My hope is that you keep reading this book and changing your own story. As you read, you'll learn *why* you are standing in the way. Next, you'll learn *how* to change that reality. And finally, you'll discover *what* you can expect when you finally turn your best self loose.

Or, you might quickly close this book and say, "No thanks!" I'm convinced that, if you do, a day will come when you will pick this book up and open it again.

Right now, if you are standing in your own way, the first step toward freedom, toward a life better than you can possibly imagine, is to keep on reading.

Chapter 2

40 years of standing in my own way

"Every flower must grow through dirt." –Laurie Jean Sennott

As a kid, I didn't notice much of a difference between myself and others.

And if I did, they were fun and interesting differences. A buddy of mine had braces, and I thought they were so cool and wished I could have them. Another friend lived way out in the country. His family had some property, some animals and no fences, just wide open spaces. So different from where I lived. I thought living in the country was cool, too. I got a pet rabbit from his family and named him Stripes.

I lived a few years before noticing the differences that were not as good. As early as I can remember, I was being babysat by my two older half-brothers who were seven and thirteen years older than I was. I liked it when they would have their friends over and they would play their music loud. I was only three or four at the time. I remember my oldest half-brother not getting along with my dad, his stepdad. I remember my half-brother running away from home when he was 16 and never coming back. Some differences are not cool at all. Like living in a dumpy house when your friends have nice homes and nice things. Or having parents who are drunk or absent all the time, and noticing that your friends have parents who are healthy and present. Being on your school's free lunch program when you notice a lot of other kids are bringing sack lunches their mom packed with their name written on the bag and maybe a nice note inside. That difference doesn't feel good at all. Or having to wear the same clothes every day, even if they are dirty, when other kids have nice clean clothes, and they ask you why you always wear the same shirt.

As a young child I always eagerly looked forward to Christmas and my birthday. That would change drastically in the years to come. But when I was a young child there there was still love. There was family. There were nice gifts. Later the gifts would get more meager until there were no gifts at all. As a child I used to love crawling under our Christmas tree and looking up through the branches at all those lights. It was hypnotizing. I remember heading to bed early so I did not mess up my chances of Santa coming during the night. Those are good memories.

As I grew up, all the kids in my neighborhood rode bikes. We attached baseball cards to the front fork so the cards would chatter against the spokes when we rode and make what we thought sounded for all the world like a motorcycle. We built ramps and jumps. We pretended we were Evel Knievel jumping over a line of cars.

Some kids did have nicer bikes, but nobody seemed to care much. In fact, my bike with a banana seat was a cool difference for a while; although it was not much of a jumping bike.

At this point in the story, please allow me a brief digression. We have an expression in our family when talk gets gritty. We say, "Sorry, Pearl!" The expression comes from an evening my wife, Michelle, and I spent with our wonderful neighbors, Jason and Vanessa. Our girls have grown up playing soccer and going to school together and our boys have grown up hanging out and playing video games together. Jason and Vanessa are down-to-earth, reliable, trustworthy, and loyal friends. Michelle and I would not hesitate to give the shirt off our back to them, and I am certain Jason and Vanessa share the same sentiment.

One evening, we got the families together for dinner and games and the adults got into sharing life stories. Some of the stories of injustice got our blood boiling, and other stories brought us to tears with full on belly laughter. As the night went on, the stories gained momentum and a few new adjectives. It was all in good fun and really helped to emphasize the point. Jason and Vanessa are master storytellers. Our daughter Pearl was eleven at the time, and our friends wanted to protect her ears, so every time they used a choice adjective, they would immediately call out, "Sorry, Pearl!" As I tell you the story of my life, some parts are going to require strong language. My beautiful Pearl is thrilled and proud that I am writing this book, and she will probably read it. So, to her, and to you, I hope you understand when I say, "Sorry, Pearl!"

Back to my childhood memories, and one shattering day I will never, ever forget.

I was riding my bike in front of my house after school. We had built a jump just down the block, and to build up speed, my friends and I would pedal down the street like crazy, then dart off the street to hit the jump. My dad had told me before not to ride in the street. Now, this was not really riding in the street. We were just trying to get speed for the jump. We were careful and we looked out for each other to make sure no cars were coming.

On my way back to the top of our little runway, I noticed my dad standing where I would turn around. I thought maybe he was coming out to watch me launch like Evel Knievel. He was not.

As I pulled up to him with a smile, he reared back and slapped my face as hard as he could.

The force of that blow brought instant tears to my eyes, hot tears of pain and embarrassment. That blow branded the memory forever. I looked up at my dad with utter disbelief, and then I looked down the street at my friends. They were frozen. I got off my bike and walked it into our yard. It was pure humiliation.

By then, I knew my dad was a Vietnam veteran, and I know now it was a significantly traumatic part of his life. "I don't wanna talk about it," was all he would ever say. My dad's PTSD affected him for the rest of his life, it had a profound effect on those of us in his family, too.

Maybe I shouldn't have been so surprised. Children suffer trauma and abuse every day. But I didn't know that side of life yet. At the hands of my dad, I would soon find out.

He would punish me for ridiculous reasons, whipping my ass *(Sorry Pearl!)* with a leather belt. When I stopped crying from the belt beatings, he stopped doing it. But his abuse to me and my mother continued.

I often wondered what my dad would have been like if he had never gone to war, or if he was not an alcoholic. I would never find out. All I would know, from the time I can recall to the time of his untimely death, is what it was like to have an alcoholic war veteran with poor coping skills for a dad.

When my mom met my dad, she was a young divorcee. Born Charlotte Becker to German farmers, she was raised on a wheat farm in eastern Washington State. Her dad, my grandfather that I never knew, died when I was only one year old. My mom was a bit of a wild farm girl. She started smoking and drinking by age 17. These were two habits that she could not shake until decades later, and not until her doctor delivered the somber diagnosis: Stop now or you will die.

That wild side attracted her first husband. They stayed married for 10 years before they divorced. A couple years later, that same wild side caught the eye of my dad, Charles Wicks. Their whirlwind romance led to a marriage. A marriage that, at the time, was taboo; a black man and a white woman. Shortly after Charlotte and Charles Wicks took their vows, they had their one and only child together. On October 27, 1973, yours truly, Andre Jerome Wicks, was born at Everett General Hospital in Everett, Washington.

I attended a private elementary school, Liberty Christian School, through fourth grade. I liked it. It was small and intimate, and the teachers were caring and compassionate. Private school was expensive, though; so my parents enlisted the help of my grandmother to pay the tuition.

I don't know how many other kids went to Liberty Christian School that had a home life like I did, but I know I stood out. I was the only black kid in the school. I did not dress as well. I had a lot of energy. Hahaha…That is a nice way of saying I was off the rails most of the time. I would not have been able to connect the dots just yet, but I did get sent to the principal's office a little more than other kids.

Why? I was more than a little rambunctious. I had a hard time sitting still, paying attention, staying in my seat, and staying quiet when I was supposed to be quiet. Although undiagnosed, I probably had ADHD. Could these characteristics have been associated with the chaotic home life I had? With parents who partied, consumed way too much alcohol, and got house calls from the police? The chances are way too good to deny what onlookers would say was obvious.

At that time, it was not unusual for students to be punished for behavior at Liberty Christian. In that principal's office, I became well acquainted with his paddle, a big one that had holes in it.

That paddle connected solidly with both cheeks, and it hurt. We got our hands whacked with a ruler. There was systematic public humiliation if you misbehaved. It was inhumane.

School sucks! I remember thinking, just about every day.

Today, we talk about adverse childhood experiences, or ACEs. Back then, we didn't have that term for it. But I was the poster kid for ACEs, experiencing them at every turn. The only saving grace was I was actually quite intelligent and I always found ways to cope with what was going on around me.

After fourth grade, my grandmother was not able to continue funding my private school. At least that's what I was told. At the same time, my older half-brother, David, continued going to private school. Who knows, maybe Liberty Christian finally got tired of me and gave me the boot. Another possibility is that perhaps the family had to choose, and their choice was David.

That meant I was thrust, without any warning, into the public education system for fifth grade at Lowell Elementary School. At this point, the differences between myself and many of my school peers were becoming painfully obvious. Playing with friends at my house became less and less frequent. I could not risk them witnessing another ugly episode of my dad screaming at my mom and me or hitting us.

At public school, I really started to notice the differences. It seemed like so many other kids had nice clothes, nice homes and parents who drove nice cars. I noticed the difference in who got invited to parties; who was popular, and who was not. I did not have nice clothes, I did not have a nice home and my parents did not drive nice cars.

Despite being the poorest kid among my friend group, I still mingled with middle to upper class kids. I was a decent athlete too, so I had an in. I just was not all the way in. What kept me on the fringe? Well, let's see. Wearing the same dirty clothes, having a runny nose, pants that were too short, nappy hair, I even had lice at least once that I remember; these were just the differences other kids could see while I was at school.

At this point in my life, I became keenly aware of socio economics. I saw clearly that I was poor. I learned that my dad had lost his well-paying job at AT&T because he had called in sick too many times when he was in fact just terribly hung over. I noticed the difference in where people stood in line to get school lunch. In those days, if you got free or reduced lunch, you had to stand in a special line, and everyone knew. This is just one of the ways poor kids would stand out like a sore thumb at school. Every day I would beg friends for spare change, so I could buy the regular lunch. Soon enough, though, I decided going hungry was better than standing in that line.

By the time I reached seventh grade, I noticed that my differences made other people treat me differently. If you didn't fit in, you got heckled, bullied, put down and called names. When I wore pants that were too short, because they were the only pants I had, the other kids laughed and asked me if I was waiting for a flood. I'm sure my hand-me-down coat smelled like cigarette smoke, and the torn up sleeves were snotty because I would wipe my runny nose on them.

When I was in middle school, a few buddies and I still rode our bikes everywhere. I was finally rid of my banana seat and rode a hand-me-down BMX.

On a day that is etched in my memory, some kids from the neighborhood and I were riding our bikes around when we heard sirens. It was so much fun to try to book it on your bike to see if you could catch up to the sirens and find out what was going on. This day did not seem any different than usual. Except as we pedaled and pedaled and followed the sirens, we got closer and closer to my house. When we finally caught up, we were out of breath. Ever notice the difference between being out of breath and something that takes your breath away? My friends were out of breath. My breath was taken away as we rolled up and my dad was being handcuffed. He'd had another fight with my mom and was being arrested for domestic violence. It was another embarrassing, shameful moment in my childhood, one of the worst. It's traumatic enough to witness that as a kid, but to see it in front of your friends is devastating. Looking back now, I realize that moments like this made me want to isolate myself from everyone else. After watching something like that, it's very hard to open up to build healthy, trusting relationships.

Not long after his second arrest, my parents split up. My mom and I had to put our house up for sale and move. We found an apartment near my middle school and she began drinking more than ever. I had virtually no supervision. My friends and I snuck out at night and broke into empty buildings. I was there when my friends stole a car. I was spiraling downward.

In desperation, my mom began sending me away to my grandmother's farm, in the middle of nowhere, for the summers. Then, at the end of my eighth grade year, Mom dropped a bombshell on me. We were moving to the farm. I would be uprooting from the only place I had ever known. I would have to find a way to survive in the small farming town of Wilson Creek, Washington, where I would be the only black kid in a hundred-mile radius. I may as well have been an alien from another planet. This small town gave me some of the worst and best experiences of my young life. Here, I would experience racism, isolation, abandonment, and hunger. I would see my mom hit bottom with her alcoholism and an attempted suicide. I would also meet a mentor to whom I owe my life; an exceptional man named Kipp Norris.

Coach Norris was my basketball coach, high school social studies and Knowledge Bowl teacher. I will forever be grateful for what he saw in me. If he had not seen the invisible, I never would have achieved the impossible. He must have had an uncanny perception, because my outward appearance and attitude was pretty rough by then. I was cynical and angry.

One of those invisible possibilities was college. No one in my family had ever gone to college, so it is not surprising that no one ever talked to me about it. Coach Norris helped me see it was not only a possibility, but a very likely possibility with my skills and talents. He took me on a campus visit to Whitworth College, his alma mater. If it were not for that visit I would never have never gone to college. It wasn't even on my radar. Coach Norris's friendship, guidance and encouragement changed the trajectory of my life forever.

College life was quite an adjustment. I had absolutely no guidance or support from home. It was almost as though my mom was trying to sabotage my going to college. I did not let her succeed. I was determined to show up and make the most of my opportunity there.

In the years leading up to and even beyond college I struggled to identify my giftedness, though. Life was always such a struggle in my earlier formative years that, even though I got pretty good grades and excelled in sports, I was always in pure survival mode. And I mean that quite literally. I spent my time trying to figure out where I was going to get my next meal instead of developing and honing my talents. I lacked most of the academic skills that other kids took for granted: discipline, time management, prioritization, note taking and self-advocacy. But I was intuitive, and I *had* developed a knack for being gritty and resilient, characteristics that I curated and characteristics that continue to serve as the currency that bridges struggle and success.

So, even though I frequently slept in class, I was still able to make the grade. But yet again, as should be no surprise to you by now, I made it harder than it had to be. I just didn't know what I didn't know.

I found I had talent in athletics, too. Track and field and football were my sports of choice. I was a four-year qualifier for state in track and field in high school, medaling in numerous events. I was also a two-time all-state selection for football my junior and senior year at safety. Sports were my outlet in high school. In many ways they saved me. They certainly shaped me, especially the good parts of me.

While high school basketball under Coach Norris taught me some of my most important lessons, I just wasn't that great of a player. Imagine the shock of Smalltown, U.S.A. when the black kid from the city had never played basketball before!

When I was on my own at college, I hoped that my family trauma would subside. I certainly had had enough by now to last a lifetime. But during my sophomore year I experienced the worst blow yet. By now my parent's divorce was final. I had become very distant from my dad, but now he and I were making an attempt at trying again to have a relationship.

I had arranged for him to come to Tacoma to watch me play football against Pacific Lutheran University. This game was huge. I had changed positions this year, moving from safety to receiver, and I was starting for the first time. I had battled and bided my time, waiting the year before for a very talented group of receivers to graduate, making room for an up-and-comer like me to stamp his place in the starting lineup. I had also proven myself to be an asset on special teams, so I would be a starting kick and punt returner as well.

During the game, I kept looking around to see if my dad was up there somewhere in the stands, but I couldn't find him. I finished with a handful of catches and several kick returns. We got our butts handed to us. *But who cares*, I thought. *Charles Wicks, Jr. had just witnessed, for the first time, his only son play college football.*

On my way to the locker room, I continued to look for my dad. I expected to see him come up to me, give me a hug or at least a handshake, and congratulate me on the game. Maybe he'd found a spot to watch all to himself. But I never saw him that Saturday and I never heard from him about why he had missed my game.

Two days later, two college staff members came to my dorm. They asked if they could come into my room. I said yes. They asked if anyone else was in the room. I said no. They said I should sit down and that they had some news to share with me.

Getting the news that my dad had passed away was an out-of-body experience. Their voices telling me all this were muffled, like someone talking into a tin can. I could make out the words, but it was as if they were talking to someone else.

That night, I was out of my head with grief and anger. I borrowed a friend's car to drive home, and I drove hard and angry. At one point I tried to pass illegally and came very close to hitting another car head on. When I got to the farm, my mom was there and she was in hysterics.

I would soon learn that my dad had committed suicide. I would also learn that he had committed suicide on a Friday, the day before he was to come watch me play.

His death started me on a destructive downward spiral. I had never drunk alcohol, but after he died, I started drinking heavily. I failed multiple courses in school. I was quickly sinking my own ship.

I managed to keep things afloat just enough to excel in athletics and to narrowly pass classes. I ended my career at Whitworth College as one of just 23 athletes at that time to have lettered all four years in two different sports in the history of the college.

But I was further than ever from the human being I wanted to be. I did not know who I was or what I stood for. And I was far from being proud to be Andre Wicks. I was angrier than ever. I was meaner than ever. I had a foul mouth and an even more foul attitude. I saw my friends getting opportunities, excelling in school, taking vacations and getting the girls. I saw them getting all the breaks. *Why didn't any of the breaks go my way?*

Little did I know at the time that breaks would not come my way on their own. Like most people; like you, perhaps, I underestimated the power we have to make our own lucky breaks… or lose them.

One huge lucky break did go my way, though, and that was meeting Michelle Mack, my beautiful, kind, caring and incredible future wife.

I was unbelievably lucky to have found her, but I don't know that she was as lucky, at least not yet, to have found such a broken soul as me. Like my coach, Michelle, saw the invisible possibilities that I could not see. Somehow, she knew the man I was on my slow and painful way to becoming, even though I could not see it myself. She patiently waited while I spent years becoming a better communicator, a better father and a better husband. All the while, she has been there, supporting me as I worked to become my best self. Even into adulthood, even with all the focus I placed on improving myself, I still had glaring shortcomings. I still experienced things that bewildered me: restlessness, discontentment, lack of joy. What was standing in my way? As you already know, the answer was not *what*; it was *who*. The problem was me.

Most of us can relate to the struggle to find balance in life. I believe the real problem is that we haven't found the right *alignment*. We chase our tails in all kinds of different directions, and we end up imbalanced and misaligned.

Instead of that fruitless chase, what if we considered our lives as a Venn diagram? You know, find that place where all the circles intersect?

I finally saw the light, somewhere around my 40th birthday. I knew exactly how my Venn diagram looked. For me, those three circles are my personal values, professional values and spiritual values. At where those circles intersect, at the core of everything I value, is service to others.

Almost in a flash, I realized that my purpose, my true gift, was helping others become *their* best self.

I was absolutely thrilled to have come to that realization, and I can honestly say, since that day I have never wavered from that being my gift; a gift worthy of sharing with pride. I am incredibly grateful to have discovered what so many people search for all their lives. Finding my center and my balance has brought me an incredible sense of peace, joy, strength, confidence, poise and discernment.

I spent a couple years riding the high of this realization; but then another realization brought that ride to a screeching halt.

Wait a minute! If I am going to help others become their best self, don't I also have to become my *best self?*

And that is when the heavens opened and I had the real ah-ha moment. That is when I admitted honestly to myself that the problem was me.

That admission was difficult. It may be a difficult admission for you, too. It is like any other glaring problem that you know exists, but you ignore the truth. Only when we admit the problem exists can we even begin to create a solution. Academy Award nominee and Grammy Award winning actor and musician, Will Smith, has a brilliant way to put it:

"We have to make decisions that are in our own best interest. Most of the world does not do that. Every day we are choosing stuff that is not in our own best interest. So, if the world is attacking you and the world wants to fight you and the world wants to hold you down, and you're going to kick *yourself* in the balls? You're going to stop yourself from getting what you dream?"

And isn't that the truth? If you are fortunate enough, you will find out that many other people go through their own shit in life, *(sorry, Pearl!)*. At these points in life, let go of the guilt and shame that is causing you to avoid admitting you are standing in your own way. When that time comes a switch flips, and you are changed. Otherwise, it's like trying to get out a door that is stuck cracked open - when it is intended to be wide open - only to find out what is keeping the door only cracked open is you pushing on the door from the other side.

I lived 40 years before the man on the other side of that door stepped to the side. Do you really want to wait that long? How bad do you want all those things in life you dream about? How long will you wait until you step out of your own way?

Remember Coach Norris?

In 2019, while speaking at the first-ever Institute for Fostering Resilient Learners, I shared my story. I delivered a keynote speech to open the second day of the workshop, titled "What is Standing in the Way?" It was the initial inspiration for this book.

For some reason, I shared more detail than I ever had before, including the actual name of the coach who changed my life.

The speech got a nice ovation and many people approached me afterwards, including one young woman who came up with a smile.

"I'm Coach Norris's niece!"

She handed me a piece of paper that said Kipp Norris, along with his phone number.

During my keynote, she'd texted Coach and asked, *Do you know an Andre Wicks? He is talking about you!*

As soon as possible, I texted Coach. Within minutes he texted back, and a couple minutes later we were talking on the phone. I can't begin to describe how nice it was to hear his voice. It was like I had stepped back in time, it was like I was in high school again; only, the very best parts of high school.

It was the first time since high school graduation that I'd had any contact with him. Over the ensuing years, I'd often wondered about him. I had no idea if I would ever get to share my gratitude. I wanted to tell him that I'd finally come to believe in myself, in the me he had recognized all those years ago.

And now I had that chance. We had so much to catch up on. He had moved to Alaska with his wife the year I graduated from high school, where they started and raised a family. I was happy to hear he was still teaching and coaching; still impacting kids the same way he impacted me. I was excited to tell him about the man I had become; well, the man I was still becoming. I was even more excited to show him the new me. Coach said he was coming to my current town of Spokane, Washington for Thanksgiving, so we made a plan to meet.

As the time drew closer, my anticipation grew. By the time I pulled into the parking lot at Twigs, the restaurant where we were meeting, it was like slow motion. I had built this moment up so much, telling my wife and kids all the stories of Coach, and Wilson Creek and basketball. When we got out of the car, Coach was there with his wife, Ann, and his son, Sam. We shared a handshake and then a huge back-slapping bear hug. It was awesome!

As we enjoyed dinner and stories, one detail emerged that I will never forget. At some point, the realities of the hardships I had to endure while I was in high school surfaced in our conversation. And when it did, Coach just said, "None of us knew how you made it."

Wow. That went straight to my heart. I realized in that moment that all the teachers, staff, coaches, and townspeople had known my situation. They were aware of stuff I thought no one else knew. And yet they never let on; they just found small ways to support me and keep quiet. Talk about the power of human kindness.

As we wrapped up the evening, Coach said those words every boy longs to hear, those words I never heard all those years at home. "I'm just so stinkin' proud of you. I knew you were going to be great. I just knew it. And, look atcha!"

It was a bright, glowing moment of positivity, of affirmation, of truth. I walked out of that restaurant feeling 10 feet tall.

This, my friends, is only a small taste of how amazing life can be if you can get out of your own way and embark on the journey of becoming your very best self.

Let's continue, shall we?

Chapter 3

Decide to Decide!

"It doesn't matter which side of the fence you get off on sometimes. What matters most is getting off. You can't make progress without making decisions." –Jim Rohn

Today, whether you realize it or not, you have been a decision making machine. You got out of bed, picked out something to wear and probably something to eat. Quite possibly you did some kind of work, and made another host of decisions: to turn on your computer, recycle those papers, go to the bathroom, draw the blinds, close the door, have numerous conversations, check and respond to email, hold meetings and make phone calls.

Or maybe you did not decide to get out of bed yet today, but you *did* decide to read this book. And there are a number of *other* decisions you might make even from the confines of your bed.

Experts agree that we humans make roughly 35,000 remotely conscious decisions a day. That is a whole lot of deciding. This or that? Up or down? Right or left? Yellow or red? On or off?

Remotely conscious decisions include those decisions made almost automatically; decisions that do not seemingly require a conscious effort to make. That is not to say those remotely conscious decisions do not matter. Quite to the contrary; our remotely conscious decisions can have a major impact in our life.

Say you decide to switch lanes suddenly. Or you decide to put on the brakes a little too late. And did you remember to buckle your two-year-old into the car seat? Each of these decisions, especially when taken as a whole, can save a life or end a life, although we typically make them without thinking twice.

Further research, conducted by Columbia University, suggests that the average adult makes about 70 conscious decisions per day. That is still a lot of decisions.

So, we make, on average, 70 conscious decisions and 35,000 remotely conscious decisions per day. That equates to about 25,550 conscious decisions and 12,775,000 remotely conscious decisions per year. Just between the ages of 25 and 35, we make 255,500 conscious decisions and 127,750,000 remotely conscious decisions. Amazing, isn't it?

Of course, these numbers vary from person to person. Think about how many micro decisions an athlete must make during a game, often instinctively.

The point, however, is that we all make hundreds of thousands, even millions of decisions over the course of our life. Yet, for many people there is one elusive decision left unmade.

And that is the decision to get the heck out of our own way.

Trust me, the decision to get out of your own way, or the series of decisions it takes to get out of your own way, is no simple feat. If it were, no one would be standing in their own way. No one would be his or her own worst enemy.

The reality is that getting out of your own way is complex; because it means identifying the reasons you are in your own way to begin with, as well as finding the way out. Getting out of your own way can be messy. Getting out of your own way takes more than more conscious decision making. Getting out of your own way does not happen overnight. Getting out of your own way takes skill, it takes support and it takes time.

I am going to give you the secret to making that shift.

You need to decide to *decide.*

You need to learn the art of making a decision, even if it might not be the perfect one.

You need to understand that that decision, every decision, adds up to your success.

And that failure to decide can only lead to failure.

If you are struggling with anything in life, or if others are struggling around you and you want to help them, it all begins with that decision to decide.

Right now, you are making a positive decision. You have decided to pay attention to these words, to this concept, to take them into your consciousness with the intent of improving your life. That may be the best of the 70 conscious decisions you will make today. Right here, right now, *you* are the proving ground. You are proving something to the one person who matters most. And that is you.

Conscious decision making takes intention. Whether it's a good decision or a bad decision, whether it is half-hearted or all-in; we have to decide to decide!

I can't emphasize enough how important this is.

Decide to decide, and do it over and over, and you are well on your way to living your best life. Now is the time to practice and to get good at it. Then step back and watch decision making work miraculously in your favor.

I want you to approach your life with the mentality of an owner, not a renter. This is a critical shift.

What do I mean? Think back to things you have owned, and things you have rented. Consciously or even subconsciously, think about how you treated those things. Look at how most people treat a rental house as opposed to how most owners care for their home. There is a different kind of investment when you own.

It is not unusual for a renter to be careless; to knock holes in walls, scrape the paint or the furniture and let leaky fixtures run. So, what if the floorboards get wet, the weeds grow tall in the yard or the broken window lets in a draft. After all, it's someone else's problem! When you take ownership of your life, you look at things with a much more critical eye. You take great care not to cause damage. And if something is wrong, you make every effort to fix it before it causes even more damage. I want you to think about this carefully. Are you the owner of your life story, or are you just carelessly renting space?

When you decide to decide, you can begin to change your reality.

Remember, *you are where you are because of who you are.*

Seems simple enough, right? It is, and it isn't. If it were so easy to understand, people would never question, complain or point fingers about their lot in life. They would not wonder why they are unhappy, why they remain in an unhealthy relationship or why they are not chosen for that promotion.

Instead, most people do complain. They do point fingers and they do not understand why things happen the way they do. Unfortunately, most people never figure out that most of what happens to us in life does not *just happen.* We make it happen – or we do not.

The reason it's not simple is that humans are complex creatures. *You* are a complex creature.

How do you begin to define who you are?

And even more importantly, how do you go about *redefining* who you are?

Who you are and how we create that definition of self are intertwined. They are interdependent and inter-dynamic. If one changes, the other does too. If I change who I think I am, my choices will likewise support that change.

Conversely, if I change my choices, they will change me.

The projection of your reality goes out into the world around you. It changes *where* you are in life because others will also begin to see you this way.

Every decision you decide to make will either stunt or amplify your growth; the creative evolution of your chosen self. I encourage you to closely examine how you define yourself. You will soon realize that, as you name the things that define you, there is a direct correlation to the decisions you make.

Author and speaker Brené Brown says this about choices: "Authenticity (of one's self) is a collection of choices that we have to make every day. It's about the choice to show up and be real. The choice to be honest. The choice to let our true selves be seen."

Decision by decision, you are the architect designing your life. You are the author, word for word, of your story. You are the movie director calling the shots.

When this realization strikes, and only then, we are also finally able to see the naked truth. This reality, this moment, this life is the result of our decision-making.

Are you driving your life? Or are you in the backseat, whining about the ride? You get to decide. Isn't that freaking awesome? Why would you leave it up to someone else to drive the most important route of your life? When you decide to decide, when you slide into the driver's seat and take the wheel, *you* are now *creating the definition* of who you are.

Lizzie Velasquez, author and TED Talk speaker, was born with a disease so rare that she is one of only two people in the world who have been diagnosed with it. With those odds, think of how easy it would be for her to complain about her fate and to give up the wheel. Lizzie's condition prevents her from gaining weight. Even in adulthood, she has never managed to weigh more than about 65 pounds. She admits that she struggled with her appearance and with her limited ability to do certain things. She was ridiculed and harassed. She was told she was a monster and that she should kill herself. Lizzie recalls crying herself to sleep often.

Of course, these bullies affected her. But, in the end, she did not allow them to define her. In fact, Lizzie made the *decision* to leverage the awful things that happened to her into a motivation to *decide* to take control of how she would be defined.

Lizzie tells it like it is, and I always respect and admire that trait. I love what she says in her 2003 TEDx Talk:

"Even though things are hard, I can't let that define me. My life was put into my hands. Just like your life is put into yours. You are the person in the front seat of your car. You are the one that decides if your car is going to go down a bad path or a good path. You are the one that decides what defines you." Lizzie has written multiple books. She has spoken to tens of thousands of people, and her online reach exceeds 10 million views. She *decided* she wanted to be an author, she *decided* she wanted to be a motivational speaker. What would have happened if she *decided* otherwise? What would have happened if she *decided* to let others define her?

Whether we like it or not, it is us. We decide. We decide to decide. Or we do not.

What will you choose? What choices will you make and how will they align with the person you envision yourself wanting to become?

Have you ever thrown a boomerang? What an amazing invention! Especially the returning boomerang, believed to be created by the aboriginal Australians. This remarkable device provides the perfect metaphor for our decisions.

Perfect the toss, and you can train the boomerang to return. A well-thrown boomerang will find its way right back to the hand it was thrown. Every time I've done it, it seems impossible to believe. Plus, it takes a lot of practice to hone a skill like that.

I like to think of life as a game of boomerangs. The words, deeds, thoughts and actions that we throw out return to us with astonishing accuracy. They fly back to us as successes or failures, triumphs or tribulations. Just like practicing to throw a boomerang so it returns to us, we can practice how the positive things we throw out will come back our way. Ever notice how something you've done a lot becomes so routine you don't really have to think about it anymore? Some people have developed an amazing routine of tossing out words, deeds, thoughts and actions that come back in bountiful and productive ways. This boomerang effect advances their education, improves their health and strengthens relationships. It provides wisdom and financial gain. It even helps them help *others* find success. Their boomerang is working to their advantage. But the reverse is also true, and this is the negative side of the boomerang effect, the thing we must guard against with great vigilance. In this scenario, if we toss out negative words, deeds, thoughts, and actions, they will come back to us, sometimes at great speed and with devastating consequences. Be sure to avoid this at all costs.

What are you tossing out? What is coming back to you? This is a good test.

Where you are in life is the accumulation of the returning boomerangs you throw. You are the architect, you are the movie director and you are that aboriginal Australian in the outback, winging good and bad into the sky.

When you are in charge of your decisions, you are in charge of your life.

Chapter 4

You _can_ get out of your own way

"If you can dream it, you can do it." –Walt Disney

I can remember a time in my life, not that long ago, when I was standing in my own way.

No matter which way I turned, or what I decided to do, there I was, blocking my own path. It was like the football safety in me was determined to tackle myself if I ever started heading for the goal line. I blocked my own progress in relationships, in professional advancement, in making money, in everything that counts most.

That didn't change until I decided to decide. I began making conscious decisions that redefined who I was, which began to redirect where I was in life. It was very interesting to be able to see and understand why this worked. I got out of the way, and you can too.

In what areas of your life are you blocking your own development and progress? Personal, professional, financial, spiritual or health?

The first step is to realize it could be you that is standing in the way of the life you have always wanted. The next step is to come fully to grips with that. Then, and only then, are you ready to make that all-important decision to step aside, open the door and let your best self through.

In the last chapter we talked about the skills, support, resilience and time it takes to get out of your own way. Now I want to offer some tools and suggestions for the next steps, building a supporting cast around you, fostering resilience and mapping your process.

If you're having trouble deciding to step out of your own way, that's okay. It's an important decision, perhaps the most important you will ever make; and important decisions can be intimidating. So let's talk about how you can best strengthen your own decision-making skills.

Making the decision to get out of your own way is not a remotely conscious decision. It will never happen by itself. No one automatically, subconsciously, or accidentally gets out of their own way and stays on the path of continuous improvement.

Instead, you will learn to make the decision through discovery, considering the options and alternatives, drawing conclusions, and monitoring the impact of the decision to remove yourself as a barrier to your own success. Whether you build your own framework, or you seek to find an existing framework that works for you, you may need a protocol to start creating change. You will be amazed how good it feels to finally get out of your way, once and for all, and to start realizing the potential that lives inside you. To begin to see that everything you ever wanted, you already have. It's just a matter of stepping back and allowing it to happen.

In the book, *Winning Decisions: Get It Right the First Time,* authors Paul Schoemaker and Edward Russo provide a framework for executing smart, strategic decisions that produce the results you want. This framework is useful in business situations, but it is also an excellent process for individual decision making.

In the Schoemaker and Russo model, good decisions are a constant cycle of four phases: Framing the issues, gathering intelligence, coming to conclusions, and learning from experience.

Consider the first step, Framing the Decision. At the time in my life when I was the most dissatisfied with my job, my relationships, and

> 1. **Framing the decision** – Determining your viewpoint on the issue. This includes which aspects of the situation are considered important, and which are not.
>
> *What decision are your really making? What outcome do you seek?*
>
> 2. **Gathering intelligence and generating options** – Seeking knowable facts and options to enable decision-making in the face of uncertainty.
>
> *What options exist? How much can be known?*
>
> 3. **Coming to conclusions** – Determining how will you evaluate the options. Consciously decide how to decide, before coming to conclusion. Use your ethics, values, and heart, as well as your intellect. Different methods make sense for different types of decisions.
>
> *How should decisions like this be made? Who else needs to be involved?*
>
> 4. **Learning**– Learning from the results of past decisions to continually improve decision-making skills.

Figure 4.a

with myself in general, I now realize that my viewpoint was all wrong. With my ego leading the way, I presumed that the reasons why I didn't make more money, why other people got all the breaks and why other marriages seemed happier. You name it, if I saw something that did not go as planned in my life, I was convinced that someone else or something else was to blame. Wow. In retrospect, it seems terribly self-centered and arrogant. My viewpoint was skewed, and so all my decisions were framed badly.

What I needed was a dose of humility, and I got it.

I mentioned the story of my failed promotion earlier, but I want to give you the details so you can learn from my mistakes.

After 13 years of teaching in the classroom, I decided I wanted to pursue school leadership and become an administrator. At this point in my life, things seemed to be going well. I was charismatic and I had a full toolbox of skills and talents that I was certain made me quite marketable for leadership. Many people encouraged me to pursue administration. At first, I was apprehensive and I didn't know if it was for me or not. However, the longer I taught and coached, the more my desire for leadership grew. I wanted to position myself in a way that would allow me to influence even more change.

While teaching and coaching at Lewis and Clark High School, I enrolled in a school administration program at Eastern Washington University that would take about a year of coursework followed by a year of internships. During this time, one of my athletes was the son of one of the school district's elementary school directors. Both the young man and his mother are wonderful people. In fact, I think I learned more about myself from working with that young man than I ever could offer in return. To this day, I value the relationships forged with his family.

During my internship, that school director and friend suggested that I focus on pursuing either elementary or secondary administration. She even placed and trusted me in the role of substitute principal when a principal was out of their building. She also provided an opportunity for me to be a long-term substitute for an elementary assistant principal who was going on maternity leave. My principal at Lewis and Clark High School pulled me aside one day.

"You know, Andre," he said. "Not only are opportunities like that uncommon, they are unheard of."

Getting this type of special treatment made me feel like I was on top of the world, and gave me a huge boost in confidence. The staff of the elementary school where I'd served as the interim assistant principal threw me a going-away party. Afterward, my school director friend wanted to talk to me.

"Listen," she said. "I want you to know that I have never seen such a show of support from a school staff. I will advocate for whatever position you want in school administration." Needless to say, all of these affirmations stroked my precious ego; so much so that my viewpoint became skewed. I didn't even realize it until it was too late.

My decision was not framed correctly.

After my one short year of interning, I was convinced I was good and ready to be a principal. As I look back now, that notion is hilarious. Nevertheless, I applied for a full-time elementary assistant principal position. I knew I would get that interview, and I assumed it did not matter after that. I told myself that I was a shoe-in. I told myself that because my school director friend, my biggest advocate and the mother of one of my favorite kids I have ever coached, was part of the interview team, I already had the job in the bag.

So, I interviewed, and the next day I got a call.

"Andre, this is the HR director calling you about the position," she said.

Pleased, I waited for the news I already knew to be true: *We are so pleased to offer you the job of assistant principal! We are so fortunate to have you!*

Instead, her next words came as a cold slap to my mighty ego.

"I regret to inform you that you did not get the position," she said. "Thank you for participating in the process."

How could that be? I'd practically had the job in hand! I had the school director in my back pocket. I was ready to be a principal! Because of my defensive and self-centered mindset, I immediately dug in my mental heels. When the call was over, several thoughts went through my head in rapid succession:

Who is this person to tell me I am not ready?

Who are they to tell me I did not interview well?

Do they know who I am?

I was in my own way and I didn't even know it. I refused to admit that I had sunk my own ship. Of course it was not the HR director's fault. It was not the principal's fault, or the school director's fault.

The problem was me.

As you now know, I retreated to my childhood defenses. I became angry and bitter. I walked around all day in a cloud of my own doom, caught up in ruminations over whose fault it was that I did not get that assistant principal position.

At this point in my life, I still didn't comprehend the dynamic between fault and responsibility. It's easy to be stuck in a pattern of placing blame when things do not turn out how we want or expect them to. It's easy to point fingers and say it is someone else's fault that you are still traumatized by your childhood experiences, that your marriage is bad or that you are overweight, unmotivated or unhappy. But in that case, whose responsibility is it to fix it?

If we are going to right the wrongs, or the perceived wrongs, in our lives, we must understand fault and responsibility. Finding fault does not make anything right. Finding fault does not make anything better. Finding fault does not change anything.

However, taking responsibility does. It may not be your fault that your parents influenced the poor eating habits that have led to your struggle with weight in your adult life. But, it is definitely your responsibility to create better eating habits so you can live a healthier life. It may not be your fault that your spouse was unfaithful, ruined your marriage, and caused you to be insecure. But it is absolutely your responsibility to overcome those hardships so you can remain confident and develop new meaningful relationships.

By now, you know I experienced a number of hardships over the course of my adolescence and early adulthood; things like poverty, abuse, neglect and my father's suicide. I carried these hardships as though I had a chip on both shoulders. I wanted and thought I deserved certain things in life and when they did not happen, I blamed it on the fact I was black, or because I was young, or because other people got it wrong, or because my parents were drunks, because we were poor, or because... you fill in the blank.

On the outside, and on the inside, I isolated myself. I put on a tough exterior. I was downright mean to others. I didn't much like other people; and I didn't much like myself. This carried on through high school and part way through my college days at Whitworth University. People described me as intimidating. It was my glare, my few words and my lack of joy. I was so wounded that, even though I knew why they said things like that about me, I just could not push, pull, or knock myself out of the way so people could see me differently. So I could *be* different.

There are an infinite number of reasons, or a better word might be excuses, that explain why you have stood in your own way for as long as you have. For why you have struggled to become your best self. And it is your responsibility to do whatever it takes, to make the decisions necessary, to step aside and let your next best self get by.

Why aren't you making decisions that are good for you, that challenge you or help you grow? Is it because you're making decisions that you think will make someone else happy instead?

How much do you really believe in yourself, right now? Are you waiting for a crisis or a tragedy? What are you avoiding?

Here is another secret to success. Human nature is to wait until *when* we feel like it. As we know, sadly, that may never happen.

Instead, successful people turn that around, and that is what I encourage you to do. Successful people do it *so* they feel like it.

Want the most effective route to being successful, to getting out of your own way and staying out of your way, to actually becoming your best ally? Do things you don't feel like doing!

It may be one of the hardest things you ever do. It's an amazing life achievement to get on the path of becoming your best self, and stay on that path. It's the truest measure of success there is. And none of it comes easy.

Becoming your best self is not like microwave popcorn. Becoming your best self is not like drive-through fast food. There is no life hack or shortcut. No way. Instead, it's making that first difficult decision. Then the next decision, and on and on, one good decision aligning with another in your process of continuous improvement. Some of the improvements will be subtle, while others will be fundamental, even monumental shifts. What are your watershed moments so far in life? Looking forward, what might they be? We think of watershed moments as points in time that change everything. In U.S. history, they would include man landing on the moon, the attacks of 9/11 and the election of our first black president. These moments changed history forever. Each watershed moment became a catalyst for ongoing, perpetual change.

Looking back at my own life, I can see these watershed moments clearly in retrospect. After each one, my life took a major change in direction. When you have a watershed moment, nothing about you before the moment will ever be the same, and nothing about you afterwards will ever be the same, either. These moments set you up to land on the path of continuous improvement. The key is recognizing those moments in your own life. When it comes to history, watershed moments are undeniable. They are newsworthy; etched in time and archived, revisited and recounted. Personal watershed moments can certainly be powerful and symbolic. They may include a very public event. Yet personal watershed moments may also be subtle and unassuming. Wisdom and life experience will tell you to anticipate these subtle moments so you can recognize them when they happen.

One of my biggest watershed moments came from reading a book called *Season of Life* by Joe Ehrmann, a former NFL football star. There I learned a lesson that changed my work, my relationships and my life forever.

As you know by now, I did not have loving parents. My father was abusive and my mother was not nurturing. Substance abuse and, likely, being the subject of poor parenting, themselves left them inadequately prepared to provide me a healthy space to grow up. I would never learn from my parents what it looked like, sounded like and felt like to develop loving and healthy relationships. Instead, I nearly followed in their footsteps toward destructive relationships and family life of my own. By the grace of God I met my wife, Michelle, and she patiently helped me change that paradigm. Thanks to Michelle, I was able, little by little, to let down my guard and actually feel emotions other than anger. Brick by brick, she sledged away at my self-imposed wall of fear and anger so my better self could finally climb through. This was tough work, my friends. I suppose it was like any sort of strenuous physical training when you have been sitting on your butt for years. It was painful and I wanted very much to quit.

For years I was reluctant to let anyone else in, including family, friends, co-workers, my students and my athletes. Not only was I standing in the way of letting my best self by, I was also standing in the way of letting others in. It's a sad reality that, in my adolescent life, my early adulthood and my first years of teaching and coaching, many of the people I interacted with on a regular basis never got the best I could offer. The servant leader I am today was stuck behind a 5'10" 175-pound trapdoor.

My wife's grandmother, Theodora, who we call Teddy, loves to suggest books for me that she sees on Trinity Broadcasting Network or in *Reader's Digest*. In the early spring of 2004,

Teddy gave me half a page torn out of her latest *Reader's Digest*. It had the title of a book with a brief description. I thanked her for thinking of me, but barely gave it a glance. For weeks that fleeting moment left my memory, until one night when I was on the floor playing with my kids. Out of the corner of my eye, I saw something under the couch and grabbed that piece of paper, the half page from Teddy's *Reader's Digest*. Sitting there on the floor, I read the description:

Joe Ehrmann, a former NFL football star and volunteer coach for the Gilman high school football team, teaches his players the keys to successful defense: penetrate, pursue, punish, love. Love? A former captain of the Baltimore Colts and now an ordained minister, Ehrmann is serious about the game of football but even more serious about the purpose of life. Season of Life *is his inspirational story as told by Pulitzer Prize–winning journalist Jeffrey Marx, who was a ballboy for the Colts when he first met Ehrmann.*

Ehrmann now devotes his life to teaching young men a whole new meaning of masculinity. He teaches the boys at Gilman the precepts of his Building Men for Others program: Being a man means emphasizing relationships and having a cause bigger than yourself. It means accepting responsibility and leading courageously. It means that empathy, integrity, and living a life of service to others are more important than points on a scoreboard. Decades after he first met Ehrmann, Jeffrey Marx renewed their friendship and watched his childhood hero putting his principles into action. While chronicling a season with the Gilman Greyhounds, Marx witnessed the most extraordinary sports program he'd ever seen, where players say "I love you" to each other and coaches profess their love for their players. Off the field Marx sat with Ehrmann and absorbed life lessons that led him to reexamine his own unresolved relationship with his father.

Season of Life *is a book about what it means to be a man of substance and impact. It is a moving story that will resonate with athletes, coaches, parents—anyone struggling to make the right choices in life.*

I thought to myself, *Damn, I should read this book.* And so I did. *Season of Life* changed my life, and then became the catalyst that would change other lives. This book taught me how to love others. It also taught me to be "others-centered" and pursue a cause beyond myself. It taught me that the real meaning of manhood is not measured by dollars earned, female conquests or athleticism. Rather, manhood is measured by your capacity to love others.

Wow. Talk about watershed moments. If you have a son, who wouldn't want him to learn those life lessons? Even though I never learned these vital lessons as a young man, I found it is never too late to learn those lessons and it is never too late to share those lessons with others.

I read this book just before the start of my second year as the head boys track coach at Lewis and Clark High School. My philosophy of teaching, coaching and living changed as a result of reading this book. Some of the most meaningful relationships I have ever developed occurred over the next three years with the young men I coached on that track team. We experienced love, pain and joy together and created memories that will last a lifetime. My seemingly insignificant and brief interaction with Teddy and her book review led to an investment that I am still getting returns on to this day. This incredible watershed moment was a quiet one. Many of your watershed moments will be subtle, too. I would urge you to anticipate them, embrace them and do your best to not overlook or underestimate them. Here's to welcoming your own watershed moments, and allowing them to have a profound and exponential ripple effect to all of those around you.

Chapter 5

You are the greatest common factor

You are entirely up to you. —Unknown

Not only are you the greatest common factor, you are the only common factor in every experience you have ever had. With odds like that, there is no denying the problem and the solution lay within one person. You. When I was growing up, I had big dreams and aspirations, just like most kids do. I loved jets, so at one point I wanted to be a fighter pilot. I loved building model cars, so for a while I wanted to be a race car driver. I grew up at a time when police officers would stop and talk to kids in the neighborhood and hand out baseball cards, so then I wanted to be a police officer.

I remember hot summer days and chasing down the ice cream truck through the streets on my bike, following the sound of the music. I loved the ice cream, but I never had any aspirations to be an ice cream man.

My mother used to haul me to Value Village, our neighborhood thrift store, to shop for clothes. I was embarrassed to go and more embarrassed to wear the clothes she would pick out. Shopping at the thrift store when you have no other option was not trendy. The other kids at my middle school made jokes about shopping at Value Village, and here I was, modeling their clothes.

During middle school and through high school, so in the late 1980s and early '90s, I loved the TV show *Family Ties*. I appreciated the way the Keaton family always dealt with real-life issues, and that the characters were all right around my age. There was Mallory Keaton, her boyfriend Nick and of course, Skippy Handleman, their quirky friend from across the street. But my favorite character was Alex P. Keaton.

Michael J. Fox played the character to perfection. He was smart and he was funny, but the reason I liked Alex most was his complete devotion to becoming rich. That's because when I was a child I wanted to be rich. I was impressed by my wealthy grandmother from my mom's side. Grandma owned a big farm of about 1,200 acres and she drove a big Lincoln MK V. She partied! Well, she frequented the local senior center for dancing and music and bingo. She was active and social. From my interactions with my grandmother, I could tell that money seemed to help give you a different kind of life.

I wanted to escape the poverty I lived in. I wanted to escape the ensuing doom that seemed to be my fate without riches. I was convinced that money was the answer. I wanted fame and fortune. I knew what I didn't want: Drinking too much, getting fired, fighting or abusing my spouse or my kids. None of these were the answer. People who we may describe as victims will often give any number of excuses about why things never go their way. They can tell you all the reasons why their situation is someone else's fault. I know you've heard those people. Maybe you've thrown out some excuses of your own.

Do you know how many factors there are in 1,000,000? Yes, I just threw a not-so-random math question at you. There are exactly 49 factors, or divisors, for the number 1,000,000. But there is only one common factor that is a divisor for all numbers. The number one. There is only one common factor for all your life's experiences, too. You.

Although contrary to basic math, the number one is actually the *greatest* common factor when it comes to your life. You see, there is only one common factor when it comes to every life experience you have ever had and ever will have. In the sense of factors that are most occurring, the most occurring factor is the one and only you.

Let's take a look at this in our own lives. I want you to take out a piece of paper, right now, and make two lists. The first will be 10 failures you have experienced in life. The second list will be 10 successes. They do not have to be in chronological order.

Here are my lists:

Failures

1. Failing my first written driver's exam
2. Not making varsity football my freshman year in high school
3. Getting second in all-city in the 50m dash in 5th grade

4. Not making it into the gifted program in elementary school
5. Getting bad credit because of unpaid bills in college
6. Racking up several parking tickets
7. Earning an F in multiple classes in college
8. Letting my anger get the best of me
9. Allowing my teaching certificate to lapse
10. Not getting selected for a planning principal position (on my first attempt)

Successes
1. Raising four wonderful children
2. Celebrating 24 wedding anniversaries (and counting, as of 2020)
3. Being the first in my family to graduate from college
4. Earning multiple degrees
5. Coaching multiple state champions
6. Purchasing a home
7. Getting out of poverty
8. Being selected for a planning principal position (on my second attempt)
9. Helping others become their best self
10. Publishing a book

Take a good look at both of your lists. Who is the one person who has played a part in every single failure and every single success? That person is you. Truth is, you are undoubtedly the greatest common factor in the story of your life.

Take a moment and really let that sink in.

Everything that has ever happened, and everything that will happen, is directly related to the choices you make. The faults and the triumphs all boil down to one little three letter word: you.

This understanding means everything.

Of course there are always multiple forces at play in any situation. And of course you can't control all those things. You can't predict every outcome. But the one thing you can always be certain of is that *you* are the prime character in your own life story. *You* will always be a factor in every situation you ever experience. And you are the only factor you will *always* have control over. I love that!

Once you understand that you are the greatest factor in every situation you will ever encounter, then something else becomes crystal clear. Do you want to be your very best self in every one of those situations, those encounters, those challenges and opportunities that will be coming your way?

Do you want to be a superhero for family, your friends, the world around you?

Do you want to achieve success, live a happy and fulfilled life and help others do the same?

If so, then the answer is right under your nose.

The secret to every one of those good things is you.

And that means it's time to start developing yourself, big time. That means it's time to stop making excuses and start building. That means it's time to put all the time, effort and resources you can muster into building yourself into a better version of you.

And I'm going to help show you the way.

Words to Remember

1. Owners vs. renters, page 37
2. You are where you are because of who you are, page 6 & page 38
3. Fault vs. Responsibility, page 49
4. You are the greatest common factor, page 57

Call to Action

By now, you know the answer to the question: who is standing in the way? I gave you the twist right up front; you are the problem and you are the solution. That understanding is vital to maximizing your growth as you move forward. But without action, that understanding has no meaning. So I am asking you to contemplate your own thoughtful answers to the following questions. Really take your time. Write down your answers. This work will benefit you immensely.

1. Was it hard for you to come to grips with the fact that you are standing in the way? Why was that hard for you? Did you already know, but you have been in denial?

2. Understanding the story behind a problem is a requisite for creating a solution. What is the story behind you standing in your own way?

3. As you examine your decision-making, what do you notice about how what you do and how/if it aligns with who you want to become?

4. Chapter 4 highlights processes for decision-making. It is time to practice that. All of us make decisions; this chapter aims to help you make better decisions. What decision has been looming over you? How can you use this knowledge to help you make a move?

5. You now recognize that you are the only person that has been part of every success and every failure in your life. This is great news! Are there trends or similarities among your greatest successes and your epic failures? What should you keep doing, stop doing or improve how you are doing?

NOTES:

Part II: *Why* are you standing in the way?

Chapter 6

Making the most of trauma

"I'm not confused, I'm well mixed." –Robert Frost

I had what I would consider a traumatic childhood.

That means I had a number of things happen to me that experts would categorize as traumatic events. If I happen to share any details about that time of my life, no one argues the trauma I lived in and lived through. Even other people who have experienced significant trauma agree.

"Yeah Andre," they say. "Your childhood was pretty shitty."

Sorry, Pearl!

I feel fortunate to have made it through alive. The statistics are grim for boys like me: African American kids from alcoholic, drug taking, abusive families. Toss in divorce, domestic violence and poverty and it's the perfect storm. At best, I was destined to repeat the cycle. At worst, I should be dead or in prison by now. I am grateful that I met some amazing people, learned that my fate was ultimately in my own hands, and chose to do the right thing.

But here's the more significant truth. It's not just that I feel fortunate for the sake of being alive; more importantly, I feel fortunate because I have learned how to leverage those experiences to be exactly where I am today. My trauma eventually made me gritty, resilient, empathetic, wise, more loving, more joyful and more at peace. Imagine that!

It has been my good fortune to speak publicly to schools across America about how to foster resilience in the face of trauma. I teach teachers, counselors and administrators how to understand trauma; to be what we call trauma informed. We talk about strategies for improving achievement and bettering lives in kids who have experienced trauma. I also speak to school and district level administrators about trauma-informed leadership.

You want to know something very interesting? Every time I speak about trauma, no matter where I am or whom I am speaking to, I ask a question, "Who here has ever experienced trauma?"

What's amazing is that everyone raises a hand. Every single person, every single time. At some point, every one of us will experience trauma to some degree.

Trauma has its place in our life story. Indeed, trauma plays a leading role. If it were not for trauma, most of us would not be nearly as likely to get in our own way. Trauma makes us set up barriers, towering, impenetrable barriers, right in front of our best self. Those barriers block our vision of what wonderful things might be. They block our progress along life's path. They hold us back from the wonderful things in life that lay ahead.

The more trauma we experience, the more barriers we tend to stack in front of ourselves.

This trauma and the resulting barriers are particularly daunting for children. If a child has experienced significant trauma by their middle school years, they are very likely to feel hopeless, distrustful, alone and afraid. That child is certainly unlikely to realize there is a way over, around, under or through the barriers that stand in front of them.

In the education and non-profit sectors, we use the term Adverse Childhood Experiences (ACEs). Business and private sectors may not be as familiar with the term, but are certainly just as affected. ACEs are potentially traumatic events that occur in childhood. These could include physical, mental, and/or sexual abuse; physical and/or emotional neglect; and household dysfunctions like mental illness/suicide, incarceration, domestic abuse, substance abuse, and/or divorce.

Adverse Childhood Experiences are linked to a number of adverse health conditions in adulthood. Not only do ACEs have an adverse effect on a person's adult life; studies prove that the adverse effects are much worse than originally thought. Those effects include risky health behaviors, chronic health conditions, low life potential and early death.

As the number of ACEs increases, so does the risk for these outcomes. If you are an educator, think about the students you work with. Picture the most challenging students and ask yourself, how likely is it that he or she has or is experiencing ACEs?

The question I always ask is this: What child wants to be in trouble? What child wants to harm those around them? What child wants to fail? Nobody! Something is driving them to do so, and my bet is usually on ACEs.

Even if you are not an educator, you still work with people in some capacity. I would also challenge you to ask that same question of the most difficult people you encounter. Do they want to cause trouble? Do they want to hurt other people? Do they want to fail? Chances are great that they do not. If you look into their motivations and their past, you will see that ACEs again come into play.

Now comes the most difficult examination of all.

I want you to ask the same questions of yourself. Do you really want to cause trouble? Do you really want to hurt others? Do you really want to fail?

Take a moment, a long moment, and begin to unpack the effects that trauma has had on your life. You are the sum total of every experience you've ever had. Consider the power that trauma continues to hold on your life today. Left unchecked, your childhood trauma is likely at the root of the risky health choices you are making, the chronic health conditions you are experiencing, your current (but not permanent) life potential or even a premature death.

The amazing thing is, you can choose a different kind of experience. You can choose to have a good experience right now. You can choose an even better one tomorrow!

By the time I was 18 years old, I had experienced 9 out of 10 ACEs. I was poor, neglected and hungry. My mom was abused and I was abused. I wore the same clothes every day, my parents were both alcoholics and my dad committed suicide. And like 99% of kids who experienced what I did, I had a number of unmet needs and I struggled to self-regulate.

Today, I realize that trauma was my test, but it is not my testimony. My testimony is not one of victimization. I am the victor, not the victim of my childhood trauma. But I experienced enough of it to understand how vital ACEs are to childhood development. Because of my experience, I have a special empathy for kids who struggle. I have an understanding of how to help adults overcome their past.

Research on ACEs is powerful. In 1992, a physician named Vincent Felitti was puzzled that there was a significant dropout rate from a weight loss program, even though the program was working and the patients were actually losing weight. This prompted Felitti to dig deeper, and what he found was that many of the dropouts had experienced trauma as a child.

Uncovering this truth drove Felitti to partner with Dr. Robert Anda to conduct the research for the Adverse Childhood Experiences Study; the benchmark for such research.

Not only can trauma cause you to fall into a rut; trauma can cause you to stay in the rut. Even more alarming, trauma can cause you to jump back in the rut even when you have successfully gotten yourself out. Remarkable, is it not?

My childhood trauma affected my belief system to the core. I lived a lot of years thinking I was not good enough for anything. My life was defined by doubt.

I doubted my appearance, my skills and abilities. I doubted I would ever get a good job or go to college. When I made it to college, I doubted I could finish. I doubted I could be a college athlete, and even when I secured a talent award, I doubted I was worthy of it. I doubted myself as a leader and a friend.

My trauma made me feel less than human. It made me feel isolated. It made me feel different, and not in a good way. My trauma, for so many years, made me feel shame, resentment and regret.

To be perfectly honest, my childhood trauma still affects me. Every day I have to be intentional about the choices I make; choices that support the picture of who I am and support the vision of who I am still becoming. Without the discipline of routinely practicing gratitude, without a focus on love and joy and peace, without the support and encouragement of others, I would likely steer myself back toward that awful rut.

If trauma is a primary barrier to you getting out of your own way, how do you move past the trauma successfully? How do you knock down that barrier and stand on top of it?

The best way to avoid the harmful effects of trauma, particularly in childhood, is to not have experienced it in the first place. To that, I would say, take a look around you. Is there any place you can help prevent or mitigate trauma to children in your own circle of influence? If so, that is an excellent place to start.

In terms of your own experience, we know it's impossible to avoid trauma completely. Instead, let's focus on two things: helping ensure we do not induce trauma in others, and undoing the effects of trauma in ourselves.

I am going to share with you some of the best practices I know for overcoming childhood trauma. I know they work because they've worked for me. And the more I learn about ACEs, the more I also understand the science behind these practices. If you have experienced any kind of trauma, and all of us have to some degree, I would encourage you to incorporate these things into your own life, and recommend them to others.

1. **Seek to understand.** Your past is influencing your current reality (there are pros and cons to that), and your current reality is setting the stage for your future! Seek to understand how and why your past, particularly the traumatic part of your past, is influencing you now.

2. **Find therapy.** Understanding your past can be a complex endeavor. If you are feeling stuck or do not know where to start, seek the support of a therapist.

3. **Help others.** Build resiliency by helping others build resilience. This will, in turn, help to accelerate your own development.

4. **Practice mindfulness and self-care.** There are a wide variety of activities and exercises you can choose. Essentially, mindfulness and self-care involve choosing you first. If you are like most people, self is the last one to get attention and care, and this is backwards. Remember, as they tell you every time you fly on an airplane, you need to put on your own oxygen mask first. To help others be *their* best self, it's essential that you be *your* best self. Some popular self-care choices include exercise, meditation, journaling, devotions, sleep, diet, morning routine, volunteering, prayer and social activities. You might find that a combination of these work for you, and you may also find other healthy ways to practice awareness and self care.

5. **Stop the cycle.** Trauma is caused by events or people outside of our control. When it comes to stopping the cycle for others, we have a tremendous amount of control over both of these things. Be aware of the environments and events that you are a part of, including your home, family, workplace, teams and church). Be aware that you may be playing the same roles as the people that caused trauma for you. Resolve that you will not be those people. Resolve that the cycle of trauma stops with you.

6. **Take the 28-Day Self-Care Challenge.** My friends Pete Hall and Kristin Souers are leaders in trauma-invested practices for educators across the U.S. As co-authors of

the book *Fostering Resilient Learners*, they give educators the tools to recognize and understand the signs of trauma in students and respond appropriately. While their work is primarily through the lens of educators, their practices of knowing, understanding, preventing and responding to trauma, as well as self-care for trauma, are universal. I have permission to share the 28 Day Self Care Challenge with you here. These simple commitments, done consistently, will provide an incredible reset for your life. So I challenge you to do this for the next 28 days:

a. *Exercise.* Promotes brain health and regulation.

b. *Challenge Yourself.* When you do something challenging and overcome it that creates momentum. Momentum is motivating.

c. *Take a cookie.* Do something good for yourself that makes you feel rewarded. It could actually be eating a cookie!

d. *Gratitude.* Being thankful has remarkable benefits to brain function.

The keys to the 28-Day Self-Care Challenge are very simple: 1) Start, 2) Be consistent, 3) Finish. Those are not only keys for this challenge, those are keys to success in life!

Chapter 7

Making sense of fear

"If you are always trying to be normal you will never know how amazing you can be." —Maya Angelou

What are we afraid of, and why? We become afraid, we worry, we stress and we get anxious. Why? Seriously, why? Let's take a closer look at fear.

Yes, there are things in life you should not do because they are dangerous and not good for you, and most of us know not to do those things. So why are we so afraid of the rest of life?

Put another way, what good has fear ever created? Has worry ever produced the desired result? The answer is nothing, and no.

Doctors, parenting experts, bloggers and the rest of the general public agree that when you are born you have two natural fears. Just two. Any guesses what they are? I hadn't seen or heard about those two fears until I began my own research for this book. But once I read what they are, it made perfect sense.

Think about your earliest consciousness as a baby. For nine months you were incubating in your mother's womb. As time went on, you began to sense what was happening in the outside world. But mostly, you had your own snug and safe world all your own, growing and developing, waiting to be born, feeling secure. Most likely, you were well taken care of as a growing fetus. Your mother probably talked to you, read to you, gave you good nutrition through her bloodstream. You also felt her movement and her touch. That touch, that talk and those songs were quite soothing. That natural bond that forms, before the baby is even born, is amazing.

So what in the world could there be to be afraid of?

Loud noises and falling. That is what babies are afraid of when they are born. It makes sense when you realize a baby is in tight quarters and only experiences muffled sound until it is born.

So you started out in life with just two fears, and along the way, you developed a whole list of them, some rational, some not. All those fears, all your worry and angst, are learned behavior. And the very good news is, anything learned can be unlearned.

Fear has a lot to do with why we get in our own way. In this chapter, we will talk about where fear comes from, what fears are most common and what fear does to our brain and to the rest of our self. We will also scratch the surface of how to unlearn fear (more on that in Chapter 16).

Outside the innate fears we are born with, fears are largely learned. There are two primary reasons we learn to fear; experiential and observed. Some fears come from observing something firsthand, while others come because we have been told by others to fear something. Both kinds of fear can be equally powerful.

Remember how I loved to ride a bike as a kid? That love of cycling has stayed with me to this day. I mostly ride a road bike, but not long ago, I also bought a mountain bike, mostly out of peer pressure. Some of my friends are really into mountain biking and they wanted me to do a 24-hour team mountain bike race with them. Let's be honest, I really did want a mountain bike and this gave me a great excuse to buy one.

Keep in mind that I have ridden thousands of miles by now on my road bike, but had not ridden a mountain bike since high school. I had not ridden a mountain bike on any technical terrain, and I'd certainly never raced one. Perfect time to start, right?

As a team in the 24-hour race, the plan was each of my buddies and I would ride a lap. Each lap was a loop of about 16 miles through Riverside State Park. My friends that are great riders and in great shape rode multiple laps. The loop had rolling terrain, jumps, large rocks, tough climbs and steep descents, some sections were very technical. An experienced rider has nothing to fear. If you did not know any better, there was also nothing to fear, for very different reasons. I did not know any better, and so I did not have any fear.

All too soon it was my turn. About six miles into my very first lap around the course, I came to a steep, rocky descent, just before a place called Devil's Down. No joke, there was a section of race called Devil's Down, and its reputation is every bit as gnarly as it sounds. Well, I never quite made it to Devil's Down.

I took way too much speed into the rocky area just before the Devil, and when I needed to slow down, I accidentally tapped my front brake. That slight touch was enough to send me hurtling over the handlebars, still clipped into my pedals.

I dimly remember watching the ground come closer to my face in what seemed like slow motion. I braced for impact, then felt myself tumble over and over on the hard dirt and rock. I was sprawled out in the middle of the path when I heard riders coming from behind. I was in excruciating pain, but I knew I had to move or I was going to get run over. It was intense.

I had my cell phone and I was able to call my friend, Jason. I could barely utter recognizable words, but I was able to say enough so my team could alert the medics to rush out to me. I had broken my collar bone and sustained two significant gashes on my legs that required stitches.

Several hours later I was in the ER, with Michelle by my side. It so happens that it was her birthday, and she had strongly advised me against doing this race in the first place. Guess who did not earn any husband points that day?

After I was released from the hospital, even after my collarbone and my cuts had healed, I discovered I had a new fear, one that had never existed before. Because I had crashed and burned (more like crashed and broke!), I had learned how to be afraid of going too fast, to be afraid of technical elements in the road, and to be afraid of unfamiliar surroundings. That's several new fears in one quick tumble!

In my case, I learned fear because my outcome was painfully adverse. Whenever we feel mental, emotional, or physical pain, there is always a chance of accompanying fear.

What if the situation had produced a favorable outcome, instead? I likely would have learned joy or excitement.

I am happy to say that I have found the joy in mountain biking again, and because of it, I have since unlearned that fear. I have ridden my mountain bike many times since. I have gone back to the site of the crash and I have even ridden Devil's Down! The more I chose to face the fear, the more I realized I did not need to be fearful. What I *did* need was repetition to be able to perform the technical elements with more skill.

Most of us are afraid of something. Each year it seems like there is a new list of things to fear. Then there's the old standbys: Spiders, flying, public speaking, needles and clowns. And most of us are afraid of failing or embarrassment.

Yet interestingly enough, some people are not afraid of any of these things at all. Why is that? Because we learn fear by what other people are afraid of; by observing and hearing their fears, your parents have a lot to do with your fears. Parents, no shame intended here, but while you are teaching your children all sorts of awesome things, keep in mind that you are also teaching them fear, which is not so awesome. My parents hated spiders. So do I, and so do my kids. What my kids are not afraid of is taking risks, of trying new things and failing. Why? Because my wife and I taught them to not be afraid of those things. We taught them that only by taking risks can they become their best self.

Fear is real. Fear can stop you dead in your tracks. Fear can keep you from opportunity. Fear can hold you back from fulfilling your destiny. Fear can cause you to stand squarely in your own way.

Say you want to try something new, something you've always wanted to try. Your will and desires tell you one thing, while your brain is saying the opposite.

No! Stop! You can't! You won't!

That is the incessant chatter of a fear-filled brain.

You wish you could just say, "Shut up, brain!"

But the brain has its reasons, and by sending you fearful signals, it is simply trying to keep you alive and well. Let's take a look at how that fear begins, transforms and potentially ends, all in the brain, and some clues to how you can master it once and for all. By understanding what is happening when fear comes creeping in (or storming in), you are one step closer to controlling that fear.

As you probably know, fear starts in a part of your brain called the amygdala, which prepares your body to protect itself through flight or fight. Stress hormones are released and other bodily changes may occur, such as dilated pupils, increased heart rate and breathing, higher blood pressure and sweaty palms. The brain also becomes hyper alert, while the hippocampus and frontal cortex play a key role in helping you discern whether what you see, hear, or feel is actually dangerous at all.

Fear has likely been wired into the human brain since the beginning of time. In its most primitive function, it helped our ancestors survive and avoid being killed and eaten.

But today, even though the chance of humans being on the life-threatening end of a meal has drastically decreased, our brains still act like there is a saber-toothed tiger lurking around every corner.

There is certainly a big difference between being pounced on by that tiger and shredded to bits, and having to speak in front of an audience. Yet our brains still act as if the threat is the same.

Say you are out for a walk or a run. You hear something growling and you look over your shoulder to see a pit bull chasing you down. Your flight or fight response will kick in and help you set a new record in the 100-yard dash to save yourself.

Or picture a very different scenario, one without any kind of real danger, but which strikes very real fear into many hearts. Say you find yourself in a group exercise that might involve standing up and presenting to several hundred other people at the workshop. You might be getting cold sweats just reading that line. If you hate speaking in front of people, you will do absolutely anything to get out of that situation. You might be the first to volunteer to be the scribe or the timekeeper to make sure you are not selected as the speaker for the group. In my workshops, I have seen people get up and remove themselves from the activity until it is over to avoid any possibility of having to speak in front of all those strangers. Perhaps they'd just as soon face an angry dog. And they're not alone. It's estimated that up to 77 percent of people suffer from some degree of anxiety about public speaking, a condition called glossophobia.

Both the dog and the crowd trigger our fear responses for different reasons, but both situations have a very similar pattern in the brain.

Fear of change is another very real fear. I remember watching my brother-in-law, Steve, endure the fear of a new career opportunity. There is a difference between being fearful, and being full of fear. I could see Steve was full of fear and full of doubt, as I watched him wrestle with all the reasons he would fail.

The opportunity was a teaching position at one of our local colleges. Steve was successful in his field, and highly regarded by his customers and his peers. But he was terrified of teaching, even though he had graduated at the top of his class, 13 years earlier, in the very same program he would be leading. The problem was that Steve still considered himself a poor student. He had struggled in high school, particularly with reading, and had spent years with the tutors at Sylvan Learning. Because of his difficulty with reading, Steve had developed a complex about school in general. He was focused on his reading failures, rather than his high level of applied skills, also known as 21st century skills. I could see that Steve had those skills in abundance, including critical thinking, problem solving and creativity, adaptability and digital literacy. Those are the skills that the hiring departments at Google, Apple and other Fortune 100 companies hold in high regard.

Nevertheless, Steve's fears persisted. His brain told him that he wasn't a good student, and if that were true, he would be a bad teacher. This fear persisted all the way up until he interviewed for the position.

So what made the difference in that fear? Steve told me something profound afterwards.

"I thought to myself, what do I have to lose?" he said.

It's so true! What do you have to lose when you get out of your own way? Will you be less of a woman or man? Will you be less of a parent? Will you be less of a friend if you get out of your own way? Will you be less of a human being if you stop the irrational fears that have been holding you back?

I am happy to tell you that Steve got the job. One of his selling points in the hiring interviews was demonstrating that he was a poster child of what that program could do for an individual. He pointed out that, because of the program, he was earning an excellent living, supporting his family and living his dreams. He told them how he had advanced his expertise by leveraging the foundation he gained through the very program he now intended to lead. Just an hour after his final interview, the vice president of the college called him personally to offer him the job. He had done it, fears and all!

His fearful brain had told him all the reasons why he wouldn't succeed; that his resume wasn't strong enough, his interview skills not articulate enough and his experience not broad enough. What would have happened if he never tried?

I am proud of Steve for facing his fears head on. I will talk more about how to face your own fears in Chapter 16, but for now I am going to challenge you to have an honest conversation with yourself. I want you to write down the answers to these questions:

- What are your biggest fears in life?
- What are you avoiding doing right now because of fear?
- What specific fears are holding you back from what you really want?
- Is the avoidance of these fears helping or holding you back from becoming your best self?

Chapter 8

Environment and circumstances

"People are always blaming their circumstances for what they are. I don't believe in circumstances. The people who get on in this world are the people who get up and look for the circumstances they want. If they can't find them, they make them." –Charles Bernard Shaw

When you examine the lives of successful people, a trend becomes evident. No matter what their past was like, they have worked to create a more positive environment for themselves and others around them. This has, in turn, improved their circumstances. Or is it the other way around? Either way, the interplay between the two will be critical to your own success. Environment describes physical surroundings, while circumstances are non-physical issues that can affect a situation, person or place.

When it comes to being your best self, environment is everything. And when it comes to getting on and staying on a path of continuous improvement, circumstances are everything. So if we are going to learn to get out of and stay out of our own way, we must pay attention to the interplay between environment and circumstances.

It's a little bit like the old chicken-and-egg question. Which comes first, environment or circumstances? Do your environment and circumstances affect your thinking or does your thinking affect your environment and circumstances? The answer is yes! The answer is either! The answer is both, and at the same time!

Our lives are made up of many co-existing characteristics. I am an author, I am a father and I am a husband. I am disciplined, I am joyful and I am at peace. I am all these things at the same time. Each of these things depends on the other; if one changes, it will very likely bring about change in the other characteristics, too.

This is an important conversation when we're trying to get out of our own way. It's easy to believe that both environment and circumstances will definitively determine who we are and what we may become. But that's not the whole truth. Sure, they may affect or influence our existence, just like any other factor life may bring. But I want you to know that you are more in control of these characteristics than you think. You ultimately determine your environment, and you determine your circumstances. And the interplay between them can change your life's situation dramatically.

I told you earlier I am a dedicated cyclist. When I am not outside, riding my road bike or my mountain bike, I am inside riding my Peloton. Yes, the Peloton commercials mesmerized me. I watched those ads and fantasized myself on my Peloton, sweating it out while gazing out a picturesque floor-to-ceiling window in a perfectly organized modern workout room. *Ride anytime, late night or early morning, just you and the machine... and those super motivational instructors.* What can I say? Advertising works!

Michelle convinced me to stop talking about it and just order one. So I did, and I have not regretted it a single day. I'm convinced my Peloton is one of the best investments I have ever made. I converted the small office space in my home to house the bike, put up a couple fans, built a shelf and a bench and hung a 50-inch monitor where I can watch my instructors. It's a nice setup; not anything near what you see on TV, but it does the job.

One of the many instructors I enjoy is a gentleman by the name of Alex Toussaint. He's incredibly motivating. Each time I ride, it almost feels as if the messages of inspiration and overcoming adversity are meant just for me. When I feel like I want to quit, when I want to stop pedaling and just get off the bike, Alex has a knack for saying just the right thing to keep me going, digging deeper, driving those pedals like my life depends on it.

On my Peloton, as in life, I have found something powerful about struggle. When I am able to hold on through a struggle and make it to the other side, I feel pride—and I usually learn something, too. I would love to tell you that I am so fit these days that when I hop on the Peloton the pedals just glide. The truth is, I struggle pretty much every time I ride. I sweat like a madman. I find myself in pain and out of breath. Sometimes I have to shut my eyes and grit my teeth to make it through to the end. At that point, I limp off the bike and lay on the floor until I get my bearings again. Sounds delightful, doesn't it?

During a recent Peloton ride with Alex, he said something incredibly profound.

"When you go through shit *(Sorry, Pearl!)* don't change your destination, change your approach."

What a perfect metaphor for life, I thought.

Your environment is going to throw things at you that you are not ready for. It will happen throughout your life, and you never know quite when. It might happen early and often in life. Or it might happen later and infrequently. Whenever it does, changing your approach will make all the difference.

Environments are complex, and so are circumstances. While you have some semblance of control over these things, you never have total control. What you always have control of is your outlook on life.

Alex's comment made me think about the environments and circumstances we find ourselves in at any juncture of life. When we experience circumstances and environments that are thriving, we tend to thrive, too. So, the perpetual focus of how to dig yourself out, of how to step up and step out of your own way, becomes clear. We need to steer ourselves toward thriving environments. Better yet, we need to *create* positive circumstances for ourselves and others.

How often do we find ourselves in an adverse environment or undesirable circumstances and simply decide to quit? It happens every day.

What environmental factors make you want to quit? Which circumstances have *actually* made you quit? Were you too poor? Did you live in the wrong part of town? Did someone make you believe you were too short, to slow, too dumb or too ugly? Were you not black enough? Yep, I'm black and I had to deal with that.

Worse yet, which circumstances have kept you from even trying? If you are being honest with this process, how have your environment and circumstances caused you to change destination?

When I say change destination, I mean you fell for it. You fell for whatever lie the environment or circumstances were telling you. And then you changed your mind and you changed your beliefs and you changed your dreams.

Alex's comment stung because I have changed my destination before. I have fallen for the lies that tried to say, statistically, I would never make it to or through college, that I would never be a collegiate athlete, that I would never be a great husband and dad, that I would never live a happy, healthy, joyful life; that I certainly could not help others do the same.

This is bullshit *(Sorry, Pearl!)* self-talk.

And it happens whenever we allow ourselves the crutch of lame excuses and limp around in the throes of self pity. Do not change your destination. Instead, change your approach. *I love that.* What does it mean to change your approach? It means there is more than one way to achieve everything you ever wanted. There may even be infinite approaches. It means that it does not matter if something stands in the way. What's important is that you decide that whatever is in the way will not remain in the way.

It could be that very environment and those very circumstances that are going to fuel the resiliency you need for the next adversity you face. This struggle is likely strengthening your grit muscle, so the next time you need to flex it, you will do so more powerfully.

These days, I actually place myself in situations where I know I will struggle, on purpose. Why? Because I have come to learn what is on the other side of it.

Environment and circumstances both play a role in our lives. But the good news is, neither play the lead role in the story of *your* life. Only you get to do that. When your environment and circumstances are hindering your personal progress, do not change your destination, change your approach.

Chapter 9

Who are your people?

Show me your friends
and I will show you your future. –Unknown

When I was growing up, I was pretty insecure. That is, once I started to notice the widening set of differences between myself and other kids. It is interesting, looking back now, how the way you feel about yourself has a great influence on who you decide to choose as friends. And on which friends decide to choose you.

My insecurities caused me to befriend whoever would accept me. I didn't believe that I could offer anything of value to someone else. I just assumed since my circumstances and my environment had little to offer, the same must be true for me. And so I chose to spend time with other kids who mostly felt the same way.

When my dad lost his job and I stopped going to private school, I started attending public school and tried my best to make new friends. I was able to find some kids who lived in or close to my neighborhood. I could walk or ride my bike to their house. It would have been wise for me to take my time and be cautious about who I made friends with. But I didn't know any better. Which kids want to make friends with the new kid right away? Yeah, you guessed it. Most often, it's the kids who are up to no good themselves and want to recruit the fresh meat.

My parents didn't seem to care who I hung out with. They didn't ask questions, they never wanted to meet the other parents and they never followed up with checking on where I was. I remember going to my friend's house to see their parents doing the same thing my parents did. They were sitting around the kitchen table smoking cigarettes and marijuana, and they were drinking. My friends lived the same unaccountable life. We did whatever we wanted.

You want to ride your bike all the way across the city? Sure, go for it. Want to ride the city bus through downtown and then to the mall so you can terrorize the employees at the department stores? Yeah, okay.

That is if we actually did what we said we were going to do.

On many occasions, if I spent the night at someone else's place, we would sneak out in the middle of the night. We would peek into windows of other homes. We would snoop around cars, never quite breaking in, but we did steal chrome tire valve caps to put on our bikes. Just down the road was a rental hall used for gatherings like a reunion party or a wedding reception. We would break in and see if there was anything in the refrigerator or use the phone in there. Despite all the mischief we caused, I was still a tender-hearted young man. I knew right from wrong, but I found myself more often caught up in wrong than caught up in right. I should have paid more attention to this. And I definitely should have paid more attention to *who* I was with *when* I was caught up in wrong.

One night, without knowing at first, I was swept up into a plan to take some kid's grandfather's Cadillac out for a stolen joy ride while he was out of town. We were 13 years old. I was crapping my pants, but I went along. *What the hell? (Sorry, Pearl!)* At first everything seemed to be going fine. We drove over to a couple girls' houses, thinking we were pretty hot shit *(Sorry, Pearl)*. After a while we decided to call it a night. My buddy and I got dropped off at his house without incident. We thought we'd made it scot-free. But the next morning the carjacker kid called with some bad news. After dropping us off, he'd nearly run into another vehicle. He missed, so that was good. But the driver of the other vehicle recognized the kid, and that was not good at all. The other driver was his dad. What are the odds?

My point should be obvious by now. It was no coincidence that I kept finding myself in these situations. Things would probably have continued to get worse had I stayed in the city. This pattern of behavior, along with my lack of courage to choose better friends, was not going to change unless there was a catalyst. By sheer luck, and I say that tongue in cheek, my parent's divorce was finalized while I was in the eighth grade. And that is when I ended up moving across the state to the little farm town of Wilson Creek. Here, there were new environmental and circumstantial struggles to bear, but I was also removed from my former associates and some of the big city temptations. Looking back, the move I hotly resented at the time became an opportunity to recreate myself.

What change is needed in your life? What might be that catalyst for change?

Remember, we don't have to wait for catalysts to come along. *We* can be the catalyst for change ourselves. Remember that!

I often wonder what happened to the guys I hung out with in middle school. From what I could find out, this is what I learned about their lives, going down the list of my "friends."

Drop out

Drop out

GED

GED then Job Corps

Busted for steroid use

Where are they right now? I am not certain, but I am deeply concerned. I know firsthand what a hill they would have had to climb. Together, our childhood environment and circumstances already had us behind the eight ball. Together, we supported each other in our delinquent behavior and lack of motivation. We were each others' supporting cast for trouble. Are you a creature of habit? Maybe you wear certain clothes on certain days. You wake up at the same time. You start your day with a cup of coffee. Maybe you take breaks at the same time each day or eat the same things for lunch. These are your routines. Routines and habits can be great if they serve you well, and serve others well. But what if they don't?

The truth is, we are *all* creatures of habit. Our habits are simply the choices we routinely make. Even if you do not work by routines, that in itself is a habit.

During childhood, I developed a poor habit of how I chose the people around me. Over time, I slowly began to connect the dots. I saw how my people made a difference in how I thought, how I behaved, the kinds of things I attracted and the kinds of things I repelled. I started to identify where I was and who I was, and I started to recognize the people who were part of those circumstances.

I started to see something fascinating, a pattern so clear I am surprised I hadn't spotted it earlier. When I found myself in situations that were successful, enriching and adding value to my life and the lives of others, the people in those situations had a certain set of characteristics. They shared things in common, things I began to admire and emulate.

On the other hand, I started to pick up on the characteristics of the people who were around when I was in situations that had nothing to do with bettering myself or others. It was like a science experiment. To keep this experiment a fair test, I tried altering the variable of the people I spent time with. I quickly learned that that one single variable, my people, had incredible power in my life. All adolescents face the difficulty of making friends. It's a tough time in life for anyone. Some will naturally make better decisions about friends than others. Some will, by circumstance, find themselves more naturally surrounded by the right, or wrong, people. But even at that age, it comes down to courage to decide. Who is taking your life in a positive direction?

By the time we become young adults, and beyond, we have all developed certain habits in this area of choosing our people. What are your people-habits? Who are your people?

It's actually quite simple. If you surround yourself with people who love others above self, you will begin to love others above self. If you surround yourself around people who are goal oriented, you will become more goal oriented. If you surround yourself around people who speak unkindly about their wife and their kids, you will start to resent things about your wife and kids. Why surround yourself with people like that?

I'm happy to say that, in contrast to my adolescent carjacking days, I have found a way to make this principle work in my favor. And it has produced wonderful results. When I wanted to become a more influential school administrator, I began to surround myself with respected and wise administrators; people I could learn from. When I decided I wanted to write books, I connected with other authors. When I decided I wanted to consult and help others achieve the results they were reaching for, I attached myself to other sought-after consultants. When I set my sights on becoming the best father and husband I could possibly be, I surrounded and continue to surround myself with loving and adoring fathers and husbands.

You can likely imagine what will start happening when choosing your people wisely becomes a habit for you. Yes, other people seeking to choose *their* people wisely will start to choose *you*. And that, my friend, is an incredible feeling.

If choosing your people is a habit you need to change, do so now with every sense of urgency. Do not hold back from this aspect of getting out of your own way. Don't worry about hurting someone's feelings. Just make the change.

Undoubtedly you are familiar with Maslow's hierarchy of need. In his 1943 paper, *A Theory of Human Motivation*, Abraham Maslow described an ascending scale of human need. Beyond the physical needs all humans have, such as food, water, air, sleep; and the needs for safety such as shelter, resources, security and income, the first most conscious need we have is that of belonging, the need for love, relationships and intimacy. Fortunately, most of us don't have to spend much time thinking about where we are going to rest our heads tonight or where our next meal is coming from. For any of you who have had those concerns, or still do today, you know what it feels like not to take those basic needs for granted. I empathize because I have been right there with you.

The first choices we make beyond basic needs is to fulfill the insatiable human need to belong. I'm sure you've heard the argument that social media and technology are warping and devaluing our society's ability to connect. Some people go so far as to say that it is ruining the natural social fabric of our world today. That is not my point here, and I value my email, social media accounts and news feed just like everyone else.

But I will say this. There is a strange and powerful attraction between the natural human need to connect and the artificial substitute provided by the hundreds, thousands or even millions of followers a person may have accumulated on their social media; people who are complete strangers.

I believe these artificial connections are not only unhealthy and fake; they are also unsafe. One day, I was browsing my 16-year-old daughter Olivia's social media account and noticed she had more than 750 followers on Snapchat. My first question was, "Who are all these people?" Of course she had no idea.

As a high school administrator, I'm no stranger to the bullying, harassment, intimidation and other unhealthy activity that youth (and adults) get lured into with social media. So my daughter and I had a talk about connections.

I explained why I wanted her to go through and delete all the people who were not first-level friends, those people she sees and talks to on a regular basis. "Those are the people you can trust," I told her. "Those are the people who support you becoming your best self."

When she followed my admonition, the number of connections was cut at least in half. Wow!

Why did I do this? First and foremost, I want to protect my most prized treasure, my children. But I also wanted to send a very clear message, and here's what I said.

"Not everybody *gets* to know you."

I went on to tell my precious daughter that she needs to understand the value that she has to the world. And that the value she brings, the same value you bring, is worth protecting by paying very close attention to who *does* get to know you.

Relationships are vital for our health and wellbeing in every aspect of our lives. But those relationships should urge us in the right direction. If not, it's time to take inventory of your people.

Here is an interesting challenge for you. It's one that I have undertaken multiple times to help me create a visual for where and with whom I should be spending my time. First, make a list of the people with whom you spend most of your time. Then rank them in order from most time spent to least time spent.

Then make two more lists. The next list is the areas of your life that are helping you become your best self. The final list is areas of your life that are holding you back from becoming your best self.

Then, with these three lists in hand, make an honest assessment of the following:

Who are the people most associated with the areas of your life in which you want to grow?

Who are the people who are potentially holding you back?

Based on those answers, re-rank the amount of time you will spend with people based on whether they will help you on your path of continuous improvement. Use that list as a guide and stick to it! You will be amazed at the results.

Make sure your supporting cast is better than mine was as a kid. Choose your friends wisely. Surround yourself with people who are constantly trying to be the best self they can possibly be. Those are the kind of people you want egging you on. Those are the kind of people you want influencing you, rubbing off on you and sharing your life. Find great friends and associates, and you are well on your way to living an excellent life.

Chapter 10

Why you have to get out of your own way

The effect you have on others
is the most valuable currency there is. –Jim Carrey

I told you earlier in the story how much I value the collective wisdom of the world's most successful and intelligent people. I am always interested in expertise from the fields of science and psychology.

Some of that wisdom comes from unexpected sources. Jim Carrey is one of the world's most prolific and talented comedians and actors. He has succeeded on stage, on screen and even on canvas as an artist. And yet, he is not the first person to come to mind when it comes to psychology and life wisdom.

But Jim Carrey has some mighty wise things to say about getting out of your own way.

In a commencement speech at the 2014 Maharishi University of Management, he shared a profound discovery with his audience. You may have seen this speech, which has more than 14 million views on YouTube. If not, I encourage you to look it up. I would have loved to see this speech live. The energy I felt, watching and listening from the couch in my living room, was palpable. I can only imagine what it felt like to be in that room.

In his speech, he talks about his father. Jim Carrey's father was a lot like other men in the 1960s and '70s. Those men were trying to do their best to make money and raise a family. They went to work or they went to war. They did not spend much time chasing dreams. If you were a man with a wife and kids, you needed to put food on the table and a roof over their heads.

Jim's father, Percy Carrey, was a talented man himself. He was a good musician and, as you may have guessed, a very funny comedian. Though Percy never pursued becoming a comedian, Jim says his dad could have made it big. Sure, I know he's biased, but coming from a guy like Jim Carrey, that assessment seems pretty credible.

But his dad did not follow his passion. Instead, he became an accountant. Why? Because it was safe, predictable and dependable. Businesses will always need to manage money, right? And that means there will always be a demand for people that know how to manage money.

In describing this turn of events, Jim Carrey said something that resonated deeply with me. He said his dad could have been a comedian, but instead he chose to become an accountant because he did not believe becoming a comedian was possible for him.

He chose. He did not believe. He was in his own way.

Jim goes on to say that when he was 12 years old his dad was let go from that safe job, which caused a significant financial burden on the Carrey family. Jim says they became poor and had to do whatever they could to survive. Again, something I can certainly relate to.

Percy Carrey passed away at the age of 67 when Jim was 35 years old. What regrets do you think he took with him?

For Jim Carrey, those regrets were a powerful reminder in his own career. His father's failure spurred Jim to go on and take all the chances, do all the extra work that it would take to reach his level of success. He made the decision to stay out of his own way. During the commencement speech, Jim said this:

"You can fail at what you don't want, so you may as well take a chance on what you love."

What a powerful idea.

Think about it. We don't ever stand in our own way when it comes to the things we don't want, do we? Isn't it always the things we want, the things we think are too big and too crazy that we dream and hope for, that we stand in the way of?

This is exactly why you have to get out of your own way. The things you really want, the things you love most in life, are worth taking that chance for.

Percy Carrey made assumptions about what he could or should do with his life. We've all done it. We often play the safe card, assuming things cannot or will not go wrong if we choose "security" over possibility. It's sort of like waiting for the perfect plan before starting something. And then one day, you realize that even after you have planned for years there are still major changes to be made to the plan. They are changes that could have been made over the years you spent making a plan instead of waiting to start until you had what you believed to be the complete plan. There is no such thing as the perfect plan. There is only the perfect decision to commit to a course of action.

I understand some of the assumptions Percy Carrey made in the name of practicality. I have made many of those, too.

I assumed I was not college material. That college was not practical. Why? Because, as you know by now, no one else in my family had ever gone to, much less earned a degree from, college. I was afraid and in my own way. I needed to step aside, and when I did, I allowed myself to realize I have a talent for and an enjoyment of learning. Today, I hold a Bachelor of Arts and a Master of Arts to commemorate believing in myself.

I assumed I was not leadership material. Why? Because, at the time I was first pursuing a principalship, there had only been one other African American male principal in the history of my school district. Once again, I was afraid and in my own way. It was an irrational fear. I have since become an administrator at the elementary, middle school, high school and central office levels. I have been awarded a Washington State regional assistant principal of the year. As of 2020 I have become the planning principal for a brand new middle school. I have even become a consultant who provides leadership to other schools and school districts. I bring up these accomplishments, not with a big head, but with a humble heart. I want you to know you can do it, too. You can astound yourself with how far you can go. I simply had to step out of my own way, and so do you.

I assumed I could not run a marathon. Why? Because I was a sprinter in high school and college. There was obviously no way I could run a marathon. I actually still believe that! Hahaha.

I did train for and run a half marathon, and I can tell you that 13.1 miles is still a really long way to run all at once.

But I did it for a very special reason. My wife, Michelle, and I decided when she was cleared of her breast cancer in 2018 that we would run a half marathon together to celebrate life. And I'm so glad we did.

I assumed I couldn't publish a book. Why? Maybe because I thought people "like me" don't write books. Or maybe because I tried writing a book one other time and did not have the guts to actually take it all the way through to publishing. Because people who get published are on a different level. So why waste a year or more of life trying to accomplish that? Nevertheless, you are reading this book.

Why is it vital to get out of your own way? Because there are a lot of good things waiting to happen as soon as you do. What if I hadn't stepped aside to let my best self go to college and enter the world of leadership? Or let my best self run a half marathon with my beautiful and healthy wife? What would have happened if I did not take a giant leap aside to let my best self write this book?

I would have given up on a great deal of good.

Les Brown is one of the world's greatest motivational speakers. I have a playlist on my iPhone of his talks, and I've made a habit of listening to them on the way to work in the morning. His voice is that final nudge to get my mind right before I work with the youth of today and the future leaders of tomorrow. I have also been known to listen to Les prior to an important meeting, in preparation for a job interview, or just before I go on stage to speak. His stories of overcoming hardship are honest and relatable. He makes doing the hard thing somehow seem doable. I love to listen to Les give his talk on being "HUNGRY!"

One of his favorite themes is becoming who you are meant to be. In one of his talks he makes this comment:

"When you become who you are supposed to be, you are going to bless someone else."

This message includes two important things. First, becoming who you are supposed to be is up to you. Second, when you get out of your own way, you are always better positioned to help others become their best self. Isn't that a great reason to get out of your own way?

In another of his talks, Les gives the audience a harsh truth:

"The graveyard is the richest place on earth, because it is here that you will find all the hopes and dreams that were never fulfilled; the books that were never written, the songs that were never sung, the inventions that were never shared, the cures that were never discovered, all because someone was too afraid to take that first step, keep with the problem, or determine to carry out their dream."

I urge you to heed his wise advice. Do not take your best ideas, your books, your hopes or your dreams to the grave with you. Make that decision to get out of your own way, right now. If you have already made that decision, then today is the day to take the next step.

Words to Remember

1. Adverse Childhood Experiences (ACEs), page 69
2. Not everybody gets to know you, page 100
3. Take a chance on what you love, page 104

Call to Action

You have just finished Part II, Why are you Standing in the Way? Now it's time to reflect on where you are in your own personal journey. The answers to these questions will help set you up for success in Part III, How Are You Going to Get Out of Your Own Way? Take your time and work through them before moving on to Part III.

1. Everyone experiences trauma to some degree. Reflect on your trauma. Can you identify the trauma that has you paralyzed? Have you ever considered how their own trauma is affecting your clients, colleagues, friends or even your spouse or significant other?

2. Choose an irrational fear of yours that is holding you back from personal, professional or spiritual growth. What do you have to lose if you choose to conquer that fear? Will it kill you? If not, how are you going to take action?

3. What does it look like for you to change your approach instead of changing your direction? Think carefully on this one and it will change your life.

4. Did you do the activity at the end of Chapter 9?

5. What is the biggest reason why you have to get out of your way?

NOTES:

Part III: *How* do you get out of the way?

Chapter 11

Hacking your own code

"As a man thinketh, so is he." –Proverbs 23:7

You have made it this far. In the book, but also in life. When you have been standing in your own way for this long, how do you *possibly* get out of the way now? Perhaps you have been building that wall, brick by brick, higher and higher, smack dab in front of yourself, for 10, 20, 30, 40 years. Now you are supposed to change? *Yes.* This section is about taking action. Each chapter is a challenge to *do* something that will make a significant difference in your life.

Here's a reality check. Many experts, researchers and authors will try to sell you on turnkey solutions for becoming your best self. Yet there is nothing turnkey about getting out of your own way. There can't be. We are all unique, and we each have our own mess to clean up. The reality is that there are no simple solutions for complex problems.

Here's a good example. I love orange chicken. It was incredibly convenient to go to Panda Express and order the orange chicken bowl, that is until I discovered I needed to cut gluten out of my diet. So what did I do? I went to the grocery store and bought the Panda Express brand of orange chicken sauce and the other ingredients to make my own at home. So far so good.

Turned out, the process is pretty elaborate, and even more so when doing it gluten free. The good news is there is a happy ending to the story. Everyone in the family loved the gluten-free orange chicken. The bad news is that I made an enormous mess in the kitchen. Raise your hand if you think I just grabbed a couple Brawny paper towels and cleaned 'er up? Why not? That is how they do it in the commercial, right? No, this was a much bigger orange, gooey mess I had made.

I had to get a couple dishrags, wet them down and ring them out several times after wiping the counters. I had to sweep the floor and vacuum that up. Then I had to remove the grates over the burners on the gas range to clean up the sauce that spilled out of the pan. And I had to clean up the oil that spattered out as the chicken chunks were frying. The list goes on! You get the picture. That was the complex solution to getting my orange chicken fix.

In the hard parts of life, the solutions for complex problems will be at least as complex as the problem itself.

I am going to share some opportunities to *begin* solving the problem of getting out of your own way. This is by no means a comprehensive list, but each of the ideas serve as entry points to getting out of your own way on the continuum of becoming your best self. You will notice that I emphasize *begin*. The journey of getting out of and staying out of your own way takes time, sustained and intentional effort. It's a journey with no end. There will always be situations where you will need to grab yourself by the shoulders, so to speak, and move yourself to the side. Just like anything else in life, however, this process gets better over time.

The vast majority of the general public has a smartphone. I only know one person who, as of 2020, does not have a smartphone and that is Ms. Theodora Deneke, or Grandma Teddy, as we loved ones call her. She is 92 years old and sees no need whatsoever for such a device.

But I'm 99% certain if you have a copy of this book you also have a smartphone. My point? Your phone has a bunch of apps on it, and each one of those apps serves a specific purpose. Tap on the one that looks like a clock and you can quickly set an alarm, set a timer or use your phone as a stopwatch. The app that has a cloud on it is the weather app. Not always accurate, but there it is anyway. Oh yes, the icon with the eight ball and the cue ball on it? That's where I waste way too much of my free time!

What most of us forget when we use those apps is that every one of them was created with code. Each app behaves exactly the way it does based on the code that was written sometime in the past when the app was being developed. You are the same and I am the same. We are imprinted by a certain code. Except, instead of the arrangement of a particular language used by a computer programmer, our code is the arrangement of the experiences from our past. Those experiences influence, and in some cases flat out dictate, how we behave. Just like I know what will happen when I tap the eight ball game on my phone. The code was written a certain way and the app is going to perform a certain way, every time. Unless...

And that variable is unless the code changes. If the code changes, the functionality of the app also changes. Imagine that. In tech land we call that an update. When an app gets an update, is it designed to take away functionality? Is the update to worsen the user experience? No, an update is intended to fix bugs and glitches and to improve functionality.

Friends, we are no different. Yes, we are made up of the impressions, or the code, of our past. But the great news is, we have *infinite* opportunities to update our own program. Dr. Joe Dispenza and Mel Robbins, two foremost experts in the field of teaching others to hack the code, put it like this:

"We are imprinted by the code of our past. If our past impresses our present, and our present is our soon-to-be past that will impress our soon to be future, then hacking the code has everything to do with hacking our brain to create a different present reality. Doing this concurrently creates better present outcomes and creates a foundation for predicting even better future outcomes."

If we are aware that the past *can* affect our present, and we have the wherewithal to understand *how* the past is affecting our present, then we can work on ways to override the system and update our code.

I don't know about you, but I'm the kind of person who has always worked well with concrete facts. I like scientific theory that is either provable or deniable. When I was an elementary teacher, I taught 4th, 5th and 6th grades. One of the concepts we introduced to our students to help improve their reading comprehension was cause and effect. At its heart, it's a simple concept to grasp.

We regularly observe others who make choices that will *clearly* produce an undesirable result and we shake our head that they cannot see it. The person who zooms by on the freeway like a bat out of hell? When you pass them a few miles down the road pulled over by the State Patrol, that's cause and effect. We saw that coming!

And yet, we so often fail to understand cause and effect in ourselves.

In reality, our lives are full of cause and effect. Everything we do, every day, causes some sort of reaction or chain reaction. Some effects in turn become causes for other effects.

Here is a fascinating chain reaction I want you to consider:

1. Thinking shapes behavior.
2. Behavior determines results.
3. Results are the byproduct of the way we think and behave.

4. Think like a winner, behave like a winner, and you will get winning results.

What do I mean by winning? It's not really just about winning or losing games, beating an opponent or putting up a new record in sales. In its purest form, it's actually winning the mind, heart and soul of those you love or serve. Winning is each positive step we make toward becoming our best self.

What kind of pain does your personal code include?

There's physical, mental, emotional and spiritual pain; and it all hurts. I have endured pain and you have endured pain. Broken bones, broken heart, broken spirit–I have experienced it all. Those who know me well know I am a man of faith. My relationship with Jesus is paramount in my life and for my life. And when Jesus took on human form he came face to face with pain; his own and that of others. He suffered terribly on the cross that we might live.

Paraphrasing Joe Wittwer, former pastor of Life Center Church in Spokane, WA; he says it well when he describes the choice we have when dealing with pain. Joe says when it comes to pain, it all depends on what you do with it. Pain will make you bitter or pain will make you better. Don't just *go* through it, *grow* through it. Pain is not there to stop you, it is there to prepare you.

Some of the most painful things I have experienced in life have shaped my best self because I made the choice, not just to go through it, but to *grow through it.* The death of my father, the death of my brother-in-law, a rollover car accident and failing in college. These all became growing experiences. Even having to watch my children struggle through injury and setbacks, which is an incredible trial as a parent. The world is full of hardship. And pain *will* change you. But you get to decide how. I want you to resolve that it will make you better, instead of bitter.

Practice is one of the best ways I know of changing your code for the better.

When I went to high school, I had never played organized basketball. I did try out for the team my freshman year as the new kid in that little farming town. The community, and the new first-year coach, were initially thrilled that they had a black kid from the city on their team.

Man, were they disappointed. I was terrible! But I wanted to be better. I wanted to dribble better, shoot better, play better defense and rebound better. I wasn't going to get there by reading about it or talking about it. The only option was to practice. So I did. It took me all four years of high school to become a decent, small-school player. Even better, the practice helped me develop a lot more as an overall athlete, which helped me immensely in my athletic career. My hundreds and hundreds of hours of practice time had paid off.

So I applied the same concept to other parts of my life.

When I wanted to become a better speaker, I practiced. When I wanted to become a better reader, I practiced reading. When I wanted to become a more loving husband, I practiced. Yes, it's possible to practice that, too! When I decided I wanted to get out of my own way, I practiced. I still do practice, every single day. Learning anything new takes practice. Doing anything better takes practice. Changing the way you think takes intentionality and practice. I encourage you to develop a routine of practicing in all the areas you want to improve in life. Read, listen, watch, talk and write. The more quality time you put in, the happier you will be with the results.

Another way to improve your code is to focus on the right things.

In 2010, my mother-in-law got a brand-new car. She drove that blue Toyota RAV4 off the lot with only 12 miles on it. None of us had ever had a brand-new car, and so it was exciting for the whole family. Even though the RAV4 had been around for 15 years by then, I couldn't have told you what a RAV4 was or what it looked like before she bought that car. And since then, I see them just about every day! I'm sure you've had similar experiences of noticing something you hadn't noticed before. This noticing takes place in our reticular activating system (RAS), a bundle of nerves about the circumference of a pencil at the base of our brains. The RAS filters information. Because our brain encounters billions of bits of information daily, which is way too much to process, the RAS decides what to focus on.

Interestingly enough, science says we can tell our RAS what to filter. We can do this by pairing our conscious thinking with our subconscious thinking. It's called setting an intent, and this is how it works: if you focus hard on your goals or the things you want, your RAS will help find the people, information and opportunities that help you achieve them. This is the difference between the RAS simply acting as a filter for what you notice every day, and the RAS acting as a focus for what you really want in life.

Mind you, setting intent and training your RAS to act in your favor takes time, but the results can be incredible. Here are a few of the things in my life that I believe are attributable to this practice:

- Meeting and marrying Michelle. For years I prayed for my bride. I described who and what I needed in a wife. It took me 15 years from the time I started praying to find her, but I kept asking. We have been married for more than two decades. The more I get to know Michelle, the more I see that she is exactly the woman I was praying for.

- Becoming a teacher, coach, and principal. When I was in high school I dreamed of teaching and coaching. It was not just dreaming. I was setting my intent. I was committed to paying forward the amazing support and love I got from my high school teachers and coaches. That vision set into motion a number of decisions, opportunities and relationships that resulted in me becoming all of those things. Seven years from the time I started visioning, I became a teacher and a coach. And after 25 years, I became a principal.

- Becoming a motivational speaker, consultant and author. (The speaking and consulting took three years from the time I was fully committed in mind and heart, with another two years to becoming a published author).

The RAS can work for you, or it can work against you. Mel Robbins, author of *Take Control of Your Life,* shares examples of people with negative beliefs. Some believe they are unlovable, while others are convinced they are disliked at work. With these preconceptions in place, the RAS will constantly scan for evidence to support these negative beliefs. And I can tell you, after playing the victim myself for way too many years, the RAS can work just as hard against you as it can work for you. There are plenty of so-called reasons to support the victim mentality if you've trained your brain to actively look for them. But it is also a powerful tool for good. Once I switched my RAS to filter for the positive instead of the negative, it has helped me on countless occasions, aligning the necessary pieces of my goals, dreams and aspirations.

Setting your intent for the positive must become a habit, just like brushing your teeth or taking a shower. I want you to start out every single day of your life by getting your mind right. Activate your RAS by habitually choosing what your brain observes. Monitor closely what you watch, what you read and what you listen to. Feed your brain with the high-quality ingredients that are vital to becoming your best self. Conversely, make it a habit to eliminate the information and stimulus that are negative or counterproductive.

You can change your code by changing your expectations.

What we do in life, and what we receive, is based on what we expect. Unfortunately, all too often we have an automatic tendency to use the past to predict the future. And that means we will forever be stuck in the same loop. Expect less, and you will get less.

When there is a gap between what you expect and what you want, you experience distress. The larger the gap, the greater the distress. People generally respond to this distress in one of two ways. People will often lower expectations or completely give up on what they want. This relieves distress, but causes regret. But there is another way, a better way. We can raise our expectations and actions to align with exactly what we want. I encourage you to answer these questions:

What do you want most in life?

What are you expecting instead?

How do your expectations make you feel?

What would you like to have happen instead?

What do you need to do to make what you want happen?

Yet another powerful way to alter your personal code is visualization.

When I became the head track coach at Lewis and Clark High School, the program had some fine athletes but had never achieved a league, regional or state championship. What I quickly came to realize was that there was an immense deficit in the athlete's mental performance; which in turn greatly affected their physical performance. And so I incorporated a number of sports psychology techniques into our program. Visualization became a primary focus of coaches and athletes alike. We learned, and came to believe, that our brains do not discern the difference between real and imagined events. The athletes began seeing themselves on top of podiums, finishing workouts and winning championships; all in their mind's eye. In the ensuing five years, our program was runner-up to the league title three times, was third in the region twice, finished in the top 10 at state, produced individual state champions and set six school records. It turns out, that visualization really does work!

Visualization is not reserved for sports. Our brain works 24/7, consciously and subconsciously. Everything ever invented began as an idea, a vision or a visualization. Becoming the person you want to be is no different. Start to see yourself, in your mind's eye, as that person, and your mind will enable you from there.

Many people have a belief system that will not allow them to realize they have infinite potential and infinite worth. These beliefs have them brainwashed. They have a fixed mindset and they believe they have reached the ceiling of what is possible. You are not your story. Your story might be your background, education or career. It might be what you do, where you live or what you wear.

But the real you is the decisions you make.

Who you decide to be.

After realizing this, I have added an important exercise to my daily routine, and I would encourage you to do the same. I have a list of 75 or so statements that I read out loud to myself. I go through this list every morning after I read my devotions and read or listen to stories of inspiration and motivation. I call them my "I Am" statements. They include things I want to continue being and things I want to become. I have found these statements to be one of my most fundamental habits on the way to becoming my best self. As Proverbs 23:7 says, "As a man thinketh, so is he."

It has been highly rewarding, over time, to put a star next to the "I Am" statements I have fulfilled. I learned this habit from the comedian and TV personality Steve Harvey. He is such an incredible speaker that as I watched his videos, it seemed like Steve was speaking directly to me! Steve told me to wait and watch and that surely these things would become reality. He said to give myself a year, and after that year to look at the list. He said that some of the things on the list I would accomplish and that some I would not, yet. He also said that there is nearly zero chance of us becoming the things we do not focus on becoming. Today, I can tell you that I am a living testament to the power of "I Am."

Here are a few of my morning declarations from 2019:

- ✓ I am a God-fearing Christian
- ✓ I am the author of the book *What Is Standing in the Way?*
- ✓ I am a highly sought-after public speaker and consultant
- ✓ I am happily married
- ✓ I am a loving father
- ✓ I am kinder each day
- ✓ I am wiser each day
-   I am a doctor with a PhD or EdD in leadership (not yet)
- ✓ I am a man with integrity
- ✓ I am the creator of whatever I want

Steve Harvey told me to make a list of 300 goals and I Am statements. That's a lot! I did not make it to 300, but maybe you can. Start with a list of ten and read it out loud daily. As you start to see yourself this way, you will recognize other statements to add to your list. Let the list continue to develop as *you* develop into your best self.

Chapter 12

Knowing why will show you how

"The art of knowing is knowing what to ignore." –Rumi

You know those times when something is wrong but you can't quite put your finger on it? You know, those times when you think to yourself, "Something is wrong with my car. I hear squealing whenever I use the brakes. And it doesn't seem to be stopping as well as it used to. I can't figure out why."

The problem, and most likely the solution, is staring smack-dab you in the face, but you just can't see it clearly.

That's how I felt in my own life for a long time. Maybe you can relate. I recognized something wasn't right, but I couldn't come up with a diagnosis, let alone a solution. I couldn't put the pieces together. I was working blind.

As time went on, I saw the problem and maybe even glimpsed a few solutions. Then I dove into research. I read books, attended workshops and found pertinent information on YouTube. Perhaps like you, I began to understand why I was the way I was. I also saw why I was where I was. The research, the experts and other people's stories helped to affirm what I had been denying for years. I was the barrier that stood in the way of every expectation left unfulfilled. I was in the way of everything I ever wanted.

But at the time I didn't know what to do with that realization. Frustratingly, while I was still figuring out *why* I was in my own way, I was also struggling to figure out *how* to get out of my own way.

Ironically enough, I have been quite successful in a profession predicated on analyzing, assessing and diagnosing problems, as well as creating, prescribing and implementing solutions. As a teacher and coach I had a keen eye for seeing the problem. I had a surgical approach in the classroom and on the track. I could find and fix the problems keeping my students from achieving academic success, and the issues holding my track and field athletes back from becoming champions.

So why couldn't I perform diagnostics and surgery on myself?

Why couldn't I see and solve my own problems?

As I eventually found, and am sharing with you now, there was a strong correlation between helping others and helping myself. That was the solution for my own squealing brakes. That was the how behind the why.

Say a student performs poorly on an assessment. A great teacher will do two things. First, they will assess the assessment. Next, they will take time to learn the story behind the student taking the assessment. Were there loaded questions that tended to mislead? Were the questions worded in a way that did not solicit the learning they wanted the student to demonstrate? Did the assessment actually measure the learning? Were there enough resources available? This is a glimpse into the process of troubleshooting the assessment.

Then there is assessing the story behind the student taking the assessment. Does the student have testing anxiety? Does the student have gaps in their learning? Did the student take advantage of extra help sessions before or after school? Does the student get enough sleep at night? Does the student get enough to eat? Did they eat good food and drink water the day of the assessment? Does the student have vision problems; can they even see the board? Are these results a pattern? Could the student use what we educators call an Individualized Education Plan? Or do they qualify for disability learning? These are a few deeper ways to troubleshoot the problem.

This process—troubleshooting the why of a problem so you can adequately determine a solution—has universal applications. Once you understand the process, you can apply it to nearly anything in life. It's similar to our earlier conversation about cause and effect, the why/how connection. We work to determine the cause and predict the effect of an applied solution.

Here's an example from my personal experience. When Michelle and I were first married, my communication skills were not at their best. Ok, well, they actually just sucked. Forget about not knowing the differences in how men and women communicate; I communicated poorly with other guys too. What an irony, compared to the communicator I am today. Well, even better put, "I Am" a better communicator each and every day.

We can always be better communicators. In my life, and probably in yours, too, this is a great area to troubleshoot time and again.

Next, I want to show you a more elaborate troubleshooting guide. It's important to make it explicitly clear that *knowing why will show you how* to get out of your own way.

See the chart that follows, in no particular order, some rather personal problems that stood in the way of me getting out of my own way. These were real life problems, and they are listed as such for a reason. Please note that the solutions are listed as potential solutions only. That's because not all of them worked. I need you to understand that up front. Not every solution you try, when it comes to making a wholehearted effort to get out of your own way, is going to work the first time. Or at all! The important thing is to try until you find the solutions that work.

Solutions for Getting Out of Your Own Way

Problem	Potential Solution(s)
Abused as a child by parents and siblings	Seek counseling. Commit to not repeating the cycle of abuse no matter how painful it is for you to heal.
Parents were alcoholics	Recognize the statistics for repeating the cycle. Choose friends that do not abuse drugs or alcohol.

Lived in poverty as a child	Humble yourself. Lean on teachers, coaches, and counselors for help. Take advantage of school and church resources.
Dad was jailed for domestic violence	Try not to blame yourself for your parent's poor behavior. Try to understand that everyone has a past that is affecting their present.
Poor self esteem	Get involved. Everyone has talents. Do not worry about being the best. Focus on being YOUR best.
Dad was not loving or fully present	Seek the support of other men with integrity, build trusting relationships with them.
Too poor to afford college	Get scholarships for academics and athletics. Minority scholarships if applicable. Start at community college. Work part-time. Take a lighter load.
Assumed the world was against me	Stop. Even if this were true, there is nothing you could do about it. It is much more likely that *you* are against you.
Considered too small to play college football	Play special teams. Develop the areas you have control over: get faster, get stronger, block better, run better routes, catch better, watch more film and know the opponent better.
Too proud to ask for help	Swallow your pride. Be results oriented. Focus on the goal and do what it takes to achieve it.

Too afraid to take risks	Get comfortable being uncomfortable by taking calculated risks first. Realize you will not die from most risks you will take.
Not enough time to write	Make writing a priority. Do not watch TV. Write at night or on weekends. When you say you don't have time you are saying it's not a priority.
Not enough time to focus on me	Make *your* time the first thing in the morning. Start by getting up a little earlier so you can fill your own bucket each day.

I used to have a hard time taking medicine in pill form. It was so hard for me to get past the mental block of getting a pill to go down my throat. It was not the nasty taste of the pill; it was a mental block. It was not the size of the pill; they were usually tiny. Trust me, I had swallowed giant bites of pie much bigger! Because of my pill-swallowing complex, I decided I did not like to finish the full run of medicine prescribed to knock out an illness. That is a bad habit, folks.

Of course, we all know why the doctor prescribes a certain amount of medication for a certain number of days and tells you to take *all* of that medication, right? Because that's what it takes to make sure you are over the illness. A couple years ago, I had a bout with strep throat. Ugh, strep is nasty. So painful, so miserable. I've had strep before, so I knew what it was when I felt it coming on. I made a run to the doctor, who took a throat culture. Sure enough, it was strep. I was proud of myself for going in early. It was a Friday afternoon and if I had waited to see if the symptoms would go away, I would have spent the whole weekend in agony.

Instead, I went straight to my pharmacist and got my medicine on my way home. You would think by these first few steps toward recovery that I was motivated to see it through. So far so good, right? And sure enough, after a couple days I was feeling great again. *Good thing I got such a fast jump on this*, I thought. I stopped taking the prescription I was given and it was only a matter of time before strep throat reared its ugly head again. Go to the doctor, get the prescription, then take it.... Simple enough, right? When will I ever learn?

It's easy to see where I went wrong, but we do this sort of thing in life all the time. We know what's wrong because we can feel it. We know where to go and who to talk to for help. We even know where to get the antidote, and how to take it. Yet we stop short of a full cure.

I know you've done it. We all have. We've stopped short. Maybe you cheated yourself when recovering from an injury. You failed to do your exercises or stretches, didn't take your ibuprofen or neglected to ice. Maybe you just needed more rest but instead you went out or stayed up late binging a show.

We all know what it's like to watch ourselves, like an out-of-body experience, stand in our own way of happiness, health, joy, love and success. Take any problem in your life. You have most likely had the prescription all along. Maybe you've even started taking the medicine and put the rest of the bottle back in the cabinet, because you thought, "Nah, I'm good."

Listen to me. From here on out, you are done with halfway solutions. You will be taking the medicine and following the plan of becoming your best self for the rest of your life. There is no end to the prescription for this cure, only refills.

Now that you know why and you know how, it is time to take action and keep taking action. Let's talk about how to do exactly that.

Chapter 13

Creating a new reality

"Every act of creation
is first an act of destruction" – *Pablo Picasso*

Now that we know the who and the why of what it takes to step out of our way and create our best life, we are going to take a fascinating dive into the how. Here are some ways you can begin to take action and create a new reality for yourself.

And here's the first exciting notion. You are going to take the same process that is holding you back, and use that to create change. All your life, you've believed a certain reality. You have made your own movie of what is true. Sometimes you considered yourself merely an extra in your life. Other times you may have even been convinced you had a starring role.

Well, I am here to tell you something. It's time to take your name off the extra list. And even the starring role. Your name belongs at the very beginning of the movie, in big letters. You are the director of your own reality.

And there's a scientific reason why.

Think back to the most important points in your life. There were things that you could feel and sense, things you could not see or touch or even explain. What was that? Can we name those feelings? Can we put a finger on what made us feel good, confident and successful? Or what made us feel bad, unworthy and a failure?

This mind, body and soul connection is very scientific, and it's very real. Understanding how it works will answer many of the deeper questions you have ever had. Used to your advantage, it will improve your life immensely.

The science is quantum mechanics, also known as quantum physics. It explains the energy we produce and conduct and how that energy plays a role in the realities we create. Yes, the realities *we create*. Once you understand the basics of quantum mechanics, you will realize that you have everything you need, and everything you will ever need, to create exactly what you want in life; that is, if you are open, patient and committed.

Quantum mechanics explains how all things in the universe work and interact with each other at the molecular level in electric and magnetic fields.

Researcher and author Greg Braden explains the world as having two energies, electric and magnetic, that influence every atomic particle, which is to say everything. If you change electric or magnetic energy, you change the way atoms behave. People are made up of billions of atoms. Can we behave differently if we manipulate our energy? Braden explains that our heart produces the strongest electrical and magnetic impulses in our body. The heart is where we first feel the feelings that produce the electrical and magnetic impulses that change the atoms that change the field–or the world–around us. Incredible, isn't it?

While the brain does produce these energies, the heart produces electrical energy up to 100 times stronger than the brain and magnetic energy up to 5,000 times stronger than the brain. Wow! Whoever said listen to your heart was definitely onto something.

What creates these electrical and magnetic waves in and from our heart and our brain? This is the best news of all. *We* create these energies with our thoughts and beliefs. These things change the physical world. That means our thoughts and beliefs can literally change matter. And because of that, what we think and what we believe matters immensely.

Dr. David Hawkins, New York Times bestselling author and psychiatrist, has pulled this concept together into something he calls the Map of Consciousness. He conducted research for more than 25 years to produce a chart that correlates the frequency, feelings produced, associated emotional state, and the view of life for each level of consciousness.

Dr. Hawkins began this research by chance when he began to see certain trends among his patients. Certain levels of thinking, feeling and acting seemed to be correlated to the patient's personal challenges, or advancements, depending on their level of consciousness. Briefly introduced in Chapter 1, Dr. Joe Dispenza is a lecturer, researcher, corporate consultant, author, and educator who has been invited to speak in more than 33 countries on six continents across the globe. After surviving a near-death car accident, he set out on a lifetime quest of understanding quantum physics. Along the way, he has impacted tens of millions of people through his teachings. Dr. Joe has a popular and very familiar phrase that he uses in a number of his talks, workshops, videos, books and articles, "If you want to change your personal reality you've got to change your personality."

I shared correlation between personality and reality on an emotional level in Chapter 1 as I began revealing my former self. Here it is important to revisit this idea; connecting brain science to personal reality.

We can define personality as the sum of an individual's physical, mental, emotional and social characteristics. Or we could say it is the characteristic sets of behaviors, cognitions and emotional patterns that evolve from biological and environmental factors, or our individual differences in characteristic patterns of thinking, feeling and behaving.

I look at it this way: Personality is a combination of our thoughts and our feelings, and then how we manifest those thoughts and feelings.

Mel Robbins, television host, author and motivational speaker, has an incredible and triumphant story of overcoming fear, solitude, alcohol abuse, unemployment and a failing marriage. She endured all of these things at the same time. It was her rock bottom.

But she decided she would not be a victim of the environments around her, and she began to change her personal reality. Mel has also studied quantum physics. She has discovered that the frequencies of the thoughts and emotions we create are like tuning the frequency on a radio. When we tune our electric and magnetic frequencies, we not only emit the energy, we receive it.

This process also allows us to change or maintain our levels of consciousness. Spend more time feeling blame, despair and humiliation and your view of life and level of consciousness will follow suit. You know exactly what I am talking about. Either you have felt this way before, or you undoubtedly know people who think, believe, and behave this way. There is only one way to begin changing this unpleasant reality. It starts with recreating your personality.

On the other hand, if your levels of consciousness represent love, joy, and peace, then the way you think, behave and live will follow suit. This is the amazing symbiotic relationship between consciousness, feelings, beliefs and quality of life. Wherever you are reading right now, I'm guessing you are nodding and cracking a little smile. You've seen it in action. You know there is absolute truth to what the experts say and to what I am briefly describing here. You are in control of your personal reality. You *are* a living testimony.

On the other hand, if you are a bit skeptical, you may not be smiling or fist pumping in recognition right now. The whole concept may seem like a wild hoax. You may be writing the whole thing off. You may be doubting every word I have written, and because of that, you are not putting this principle to work in your own life.

I can assure you, we are in control–for better or for worse–of the realities we face in life. That control comes through the frequencies we project based on the thoughts, beliefs and emotions we choose. We have the capacity to control the magnetic and electric fields around us; and in return receive the resulting rearrangement of atoms in people, places, things, taking the shape of beliefs fulfilled.

Chapter 14

When it's time to heal

"As my sufferings mounted, I soon realized that there were two ways in which I could respond to my situation—either to react with bitterness or seek to transform the suffering into a creative force. I decided to follow the latter course." –Martin Luther King, Jr.

There comes a time in life for everything.

For me, for you, there must come a time to heal. And healing, like anything else worth doing, takes effort. It can be a tough road. One aspect of healing that can be particularly difficult is forgiveness.

My traumatic childhood left me many reasons to be bitter, to be angry, to hold onto blame. And I have experienced all those emotions, and then some. But I have discovered something profound. The only thing that fixes those feelings, that heals those wounds, is forgiveness.

Keep in mind that forgiveness is for *you*, not for the person who is being forgiven. And that the goal is to bring closure to the events that caused those wounds so you can move on. Unresolved conflict leaves unhealed wounds. Those open wounds hurt you and the ones you love, not the person who wounded you.

And so, we come to that trickiest forgiveness of all; forgiveness of yourself.

In Chapter 4, we talked about fault and responsibility. Over the course of my life, I have discovered a distinct connection between fault and responsibility, between not forgiving and forgiving. It does not matter whose fault something is; when it comes time to make it right, it only matters whose responsibility it is. And the same is true for forgiveness. Do not get caught up in whether or not the person being forgiven changes their behavior (unless it is yourself). Just forgive. Remember that, reflect on it and act accordingly. Forgive, forgive, forgive!

Trauma doesn't just cause a nick or a scratch. It causes wounds that go incredibly deep and always leave behind scars. The great news is, if treated properly, those wounds can heal. And the scars cannot hold us back from our best lives. In fact, they can make us better than ever.

Think of an athlete who has come back stronger than ever after injury, or someone who has found financial security after extreme poverty, or a loving father who was abused as a child. Case in point, Andre J. Wicks.

An important part of the healing process is embracing your pain. How many of you have a story of deep pain; of trauma, wounds, scars and healing? Raising your hand, like I am? Sure you are, because we've all felt pain; but how many of us have learned to embrace it? When we embrace the struggle, we find our way through. We realize we aren't just okay, we realize we are actually better because of the pain.

I listen to Dr. Laura Schlessinger, mostly with my wife on long road trips. What can I say? Dr. Laura is good! All kidding aside, she really does give some great advice. As I began writing this book, on a road trip home from the Oregon Coast, I heard an episode of Dr. Laura that stood out to me. I knew I needed to share it with you.

In this particular episode, in speaking with a caller named Samantha, Dr. Laura talked about how to deal with a traumatic childhood, or trauma in general.

Dr. Laura: "Now, there are two kinds of people in this world. There are the people who have those big disappointments and they spend their lives being sad. And, then there are the other people, who go, "It is sad that I have these disappointments, but I am sooo lucky because I have...fill in the blank. Samantha, which do you think are the happier people?"

Samantha: "The people who are sad—but still happy."

Dr. Laura: "Yup. That's going to be you, Samantha. That's how you are going to deal with it. You are going to be sad that you can't count on your mommy and daddy, but you are going to be happy because there are people you *can* count on. And you are going to make a happy life." I love Dr. Laura's straightforward clarity in situations that can initially seem unclear. She advocates healing and dealing. It's a highly effective technique that can help anyone who has experienced trauma, and will experience it again in the future. Because sooner or later, as we discussed earlier, every one of us deals with trauma.

Healing and dealing are not absent of feeling. It is not an equation of healing plus dealing minus feeling. Feeling sadness is part of healing and dealing, and so is the recognition of all we have to be grateful for.

Another proven way to heal is to do good things. When I was coming up through the ranks of teaching and leadership, some of the people I looked up to included John Maxwell, Zig Ziglar, Jim Collins and Les Brown. I am inspired by great leadership. From a young age, I have been motivated and inspired to motivate and inspire. I have always had a propensity to help others. Even before I knew it was my calling, I was responding to the call.

One important concept from these mentors is that when we are communicating for change, we always need to keep our language in the affirmative tense. Instead of saying, "Stop this," or "Don't that," I learned a better way. Now I drop the negative and say, "Do this!" or "Do that!

This is effective psychology. It helps us say and hear what we want instead of what we don't want. I encourage you to try this subtle, but highly useful strategy. I challenge you to focus on flipping that switch. Track yourself closely for a day and see how often you catch yourself using those negative words or phrases. Then change them for the positive.

You'll be happy you did. Your awareness will lead to intention, and your intention to improvement.

When it comes to healing, focus on doing good things. I could tell you to stop doing bad things, but focusing on stopping bad habits is not as effective as focusing on creating and sticking to good habits. You cannot eat and drink at the same time. Similarly, you cannot focus on doing good things and stopping bad things at the same time. Since this is true, stopping bad things does not produce a bonus effect of also doing something good. However, doing something good does produce a bonus effect. If you are doing something good and not doing something bad to yourself or to others, *bonus!*

Healing takes intent. It takes retraining your Reticular Activating System. It takes re-focusing on love, joy and peace. Jaggi Vasudev, better known as Sadhguru, is an Indian yogi and author, and I appreciate his golden nuggets of wisdom. Sadhguru says:

"If you do good things, it does not matter for what reason you do good things; even if you do them for a wrong reason, good things will happen for you."

What are those good things, you ask? Once you set your intention, the rest will soon become crystal clear. Here's a question for you. How clean are your life's windows? I'll explain exactly what I mean.

A few months before I started writing this book, I came across a video about Joe Roberts, whose nickname is The Skidrow CEO. Joe's talk is powerful, and his message is about unlocking your untapped potential. In the video, Joe reveals he was a high school dropout, a drug addict and homeless. He tells the viewers that he tried drugs for the first time shortly after his ninth birthday. At the age of nine. Absolutely tragic. This was about a year after Joe's loving dad, his hero, suddenly passed away. Joe became defiant and unruly and was kicked out of his house by his mom's new husband, who was an alcoholic and was abusive. He was on the street by 15 and in trouble with the law by 16.

Joe is incredibly honest and vulnerable in telling his story. He describes himself as a liar, a thief, a cheat and a mooch. He recounts walking down the street during a downpour at age 16, homeless, soaking wet, terribly distraught at how far he'd come from his happy home, and wondering how he'd ended up here. The next day was beautiful and sunny, but he was still destitute and afraid. He sat down on a park bench next to an old man, bummed a cigarette and struck up a conversation.

Something incredible happened next. The old man, whose name was Gus, looked at Joe and said, "You know, Joe, there's more to you than you can see. But life has... well, it has dirtied your windows so the light doesn't get in. And, your light doesn't get out. You could go on to do extraordinary things, 'cause you're a real bright guy. There's more to you than you can see."

As this was happening, as Gus was speaking his truth to him, Joe was looking over his shoulder for another person. He was certain Gus had to be talking to someone else. At that point, he was so far gone that he could not see what Gus could see.

When he did realize Gus actually was talking to him, his heart sank. In that moment, he saw the hard truth. He saw that for years he had blamed society, his stepfather and other people, instead of taking responsibility for his own life, he was deflecting it. He vowed to change. Today, as an author of multiple books, and with a career as a successful motivational speaker, Joe's windows are clean. He took responsibility for cleaning them himself. And along the way, he has granted forgiveness to himself and others. He has done his healing.

Joe really caught my attention when he talked about deflecting responsibility. As people, we don't just reflect light. We project it, too. Each of us is born with love, joy, happiness and light. Our heart, our mind and our soul are incubators for these positive qualities.

However, if our windows are dirty, we can neither reflect or project the light. Trauma can be that grime and grit, holding us back from letting light in and letting our own light out. Gus was right; until we get rid of that grime, we'll never live up to our true potential.

My friends, I am challenging you to take Gus's wise counsel, and do these three important things when it comes to the windows of your soul:

1. Clean your windows of the dirt that has accumulated there.
2. Allow the light of the world to shine in.
3. Reflect the light that shines on you and project the light from within you.

Chapter 15

There are no shortcuts to change

"Everyone thinks of changing the world, but no one thinks of changing himself." –Leo Tolstoy

When it comes to getting out of your own way, change cannot be simply a noun. It must be an active verb. By now, you are well into Part III of this book, which means you are well on your way to becoming your best self, and helping others do the same. In this context, change is not a person, place or thing. It is an action or a state of *becoming*.

When it comes to getting out of your own way, success means change. And change is rarely convenient. We're not talking about changing your outfit here; we're talking about changing the routines and habits you've had for years that are not serving you well. Becoming your best self is an amazing achievement that just keeps improving; minute by minute, hour by hour, day by day, year after year. How many people get to say that? Becoming your best self is one of the most important things you will ever accomplish. It's something to brag about, something to be proud of and something to share with others. Change is the true measure of success, and there is nothing quick about it. There is no shortcut to becoming your best self. Real change is never a fast food drive-through "meal." Instead, it's shopping and foraging near and wide for the very best ingredients, then taking the time to prep them, slow cook them and serve them to appreciative guests, all while enjoying the process, the aromas, the tastes and textures. Instead of gulping a Starbucks with one hand while you drive, it's a mindful morning's routine; grinding the beans yourself, making coffee in the French press, taking the time to sip it in appreciation and gratitude. Two completely different mindsets, yielding two completely different results.

The concept of change means you will never rest in your progress. You will always be striving for more. Once you take the path to change, you will continue to evolve, even if you like who you are right now. Just wait until you see the you that waits around the next bend!

I grew up in the heyday of the Rocky movies. I've seen them all, and every time they are replayed on TV, I try to tune in. It brings me right back to my youth. In 1985, I remember watching the trailer for Rocky IV with great excitement. I couldn't wait to see it!

In my opinion, Rocky IV is one of a kind and the best in the series. The villain is the big, bad, steroid-enhanced Russian Ivan Drago, played to perfection by Dolph Lundgren. Yes he is big. And, yes, he is a badass *(Sorry, Pearl!)*. Drago is scheduled to fight Rocky's good buddy, Apollo Creed, played by the very fit Carl Weathers. Apollo is amped up for the bout. He's going to show the Russian how we do business in the US of A. The fight is in Las Vegas, and Apollo, true to his showman self, puts on a show; before the fight, that is. During the fight, it's unfortunately a different story.

Drago, it turns out, packs a devastating punch. While Apollo is getting his bones beat, Apollo's long-time trainer Duke is pleading with Rocky, "Throw the damn towel!"

Rocky is hesitant to stop the fight against Apollo's wishes, but he finally listens to Duke. Just as the towel leaves Rocky's hand, Drago delivers one last punch that drops Apollo to the canvas, forever. On his knees in the middle of the ring, Rocky clings to Apollo as his friend takes his last breath in his arms. It's nerdy, but even as I write the story I'm brought back to my 12-year-old self and the intensity in which I watched that scene unfold.

You might have taken a few punches of your own in life, right? Did it feel like a steroid-injecting badass landed a right cross and an uppercut combo? Maybe even a near-lethal blow? Some of you have been knocked to the canvas. Some of you *have* thrown in the towel. Some of you do not mind it so much on the floor; at least no one is punching you down there.

For those of you who keep getting knocked down, particularly the ones who have gotten comfortable being down; it is definitely time for a change. The difference between your knock down and an actual boxing match is that we have the luxury of picking up the towel again, dusting ourselves off and continuing the fight. You're not done yet! You have something special to offer the world that no one else does. Don't you dare leave that towel on the floor! Pick it up! Get your wits about you and start punching back.

Do you want to improve? Then have the courage to get up off the canvas and finish the fight.

Perhaps you are thinking, *What if I don't want to change? Maybe if I change I will no longer be accepted. Or I might not get what I want.* I have one question for you: is what you are doing right now getting you what you want? If not, then change must occur. Change is at the heart of improvement, and difference is the heart of change.

It's okay to risk becoming who you are meant to become. In 2019, I took that risk in front of an interview committee.

I really wanted to get the job as a planning principal for a brand-new middle school. But I also needed to tell them the truth. This is what I shared with the team near the end of the interview:

"I am a different kind of leader. I pride myself in that. I don't want you to worry that I'm ever going to do something crazy that makes you regret you chose me; but I am different. I'm different in a way that is honorable and admirable. In 1962, President John F. Kennedy gave his famous speech at a time when there was a race to put a man on the moon. He challenged the people of America to do hard things. I have challenged myself to do the leadership things that are hard; something a lot of leaders won't or don't or can't do. It's been a leadership characteristic that has set me apart and has produced notable results."

You'll be happy to note that I handled this job interview completely differently than the one you read about near the beginning of the book. I left the interview with my head held high. I remained confident in my abilities as a leader, and with what I had said, even when the hiring committee selected someone else for the job. And I kept right on believing I was the right candidate. I put into practice the principles for success I am teaching you. I drew from this book to keep myself in the right frame of mind and spirit. I decided to decide. I determined I would not quit. And almost exactly one year later, in December of 2020, I was named planning principal of the third brand new middle school set to open the fall of 2023.

Never give up! If you consider yourself a quitter, consider the reasons why. If you quit something that is not helping you become your best self, that is okay. That's the good kind of quitting. On the other hand, if you are quitting things that support your best self but you think they are too hard, or they are taking too long, or you are bored, that is *not* okay.

Don't quit. Get back up and do the thing.

Quitters quit because they rationalize a "why not" that is stronger than their "why to." My challenge for you is this: Turn that thinking on its head. Resolve to make your "why to" stronger than your "why not." Perhaps you are struggling to find a "why to" that is strong enough to keep you on the path of continuous improvement. That's an excellent cause for self-reflection. Here are my thoughts on finding that "why."

There is inspiration all around us. Yet so many of us wait, unsuccessfully, to be inspired. Those of us who seek inspiration and those who seek to inspire others spend none of our time waiting for it. We soak it up like sponges and it pumps through our veins.

If you are living with your eyes and your heart wide open, you will learn that there's inspiration in many of the simple things that are often overlooked in life. If you blink, you might miss them. You will find inspiration in situations and circumstances that are not typically considered inspiring at all. You will find it in both joy and in heartache. In good times and in hardship. In wins and losses. When life is comfortable and uncomfortable. When it is funny and when it is scary.

On a sunny but chilly Saturday in 2018, while my wife coached the game, I watched my 10-year-old daughter, Pearl, play soccer. She scored four goals and won two games that day, which made me a proud and happy dad. But I also found myself inspired by another young lady, a defender on Pearl's team, who got beat at midfield toward the end of the game. She was fooled by a juke and fell to the ground.

As the defender fell, I watched the little girl from the other team sprint away with the ball, on a breakaway with no one between her and the goalie. It looked certain she would score. But out of the corner of my eye, I saw the defender roll back to her feet, without hesitating, like there was no other option but to get up, run that girl down and prevent the goal.

Our defender, Tierney, did run the girl down and she did prevent the goal. She didn't give up! What is interesting is our team was winning 4-0 with only a few moments left in the game. Why didn't Tierney just let the other team score?

I've watched it happen with youth, high school players, college athletes and pros. I have watched it happen with people in life. There are people who refuse to be beat, even when they are knocked down. Then there are others who make a mistake and they stay behind, settle for defeat and do not attempt to learn from the mistake. Or, worst of all, they assume it doesn't matter, and they miss out on the opportunity to get better, and to prove they are better to themselves.

When I first reflected on Tierney getting up from her fall I was preparing to fly to San Diego to speak at the ASU+GSV Summit, a convening of leaders in education and talent technology. In my quest for self-improvement, I have read countless books and articles, listened to dozens of speakers and watched hundreds of inspirational videos. I could have tapped into any of these experiences as I prepared my speech for the Summit. But, instead I'm drawing from the visual of that 10-year-old defender on the soccer field. We have all been beaten and needed to bounce back. We have all fallen and had to get back up. We have all won and had to keep on winning at life.

We have had to get back up at a moment's notice and without hesitating, or we miss the chance to seize an opportunity. With clear eyes and an open heart I realized during my preparation for the Summit you don't have to be an author, a scholar, on stage, behind a microphone, or on YouTube to inspire. So I don't only look there. Oftentimes, I look at what is right in front of me. I look at a determined 10-year-old girl.

I am telling you, there is inspiration all around us. What little things will you notice today that will inspire you and will beckon you to inspire others?

Who are you becoming today? Do you remember who you were 10 years ago? Five years ago? One year ago? Last month? Yesterday? If you are like me, the answer is unequivocally yes. And thank God I'm not the same person I was back then. Or even the person I was yesterday! I believe one of the greatest gifts we have is the opportunity to evolve every day.

Long before grit, growth mindset, and resilience were buzz words, I would have described myself as a person always focused on becoming better than I was the day before. Like you, like everyone, I have had a number of challenges, and opportunities, in life. I am grateful that I have found the silver lining in many of those situations. My silver lining is finding the opportunity within every challenge.

I have seen an irrefutable difference between a person who is complacent *being* something versus a person who is focused on *becoming* something. Today, I have an unshakeable commitment to *becoming*. And I encourage everyone I can to do the same.

When my younger son, Xavier, was a freshman in high school, he took advantage of the opportunity to play football. He and 31 other freshman boys arrived in August for the first practice. For Xavier, this was an exciting time in his football life. Up until this point, because of his size, he'd been suited up as a lineman, even though he was typically much faster than most kids on his team and the opposing teams. In high school, though, he would be able to play wherever he could have the biggest impact. The question was, how would he respond to the opportunity?

Many of the other boys were just happy to be football players. Some of them were actually quite nervous. Most were content to represent their school, wear the jersey on game day, get their lockers decorated and feel the joy of being part of the program. A few players were different. They had a vision, and that vision did not rest on simply *being*. Rather, it was committed to *becoming* the best player each of them could possibly become and in doing so becoming state champions. I'm happy to say my boy was one of those with a vision.

This difference seemed insignificant at first, but over time it increasingly manifested itself as a profound difference in these student-athletes. That mindset governed how they ate, slept and trained. It influenced how they spent their time, and who they spent it with. It helped them decide whether or not to go to parties, or how hard to work to stay academically eligible. You get the picture. They *behaved* differently because they *believed* that in doing so they were *becoming* something different than the status quo.

Mind you, those other players on the team, those content to simply *be* a player, improved too. By default, if they showed up, practiced, played and stayed in the program for four years they got better. However, the players who were committed to a process of what they believed would result in them becoming state champions got better, too. Exponentially better. They became smarter, bigger, faster and stronger, and they never wavered from being on pace for on-time graduation.

Xavier and his team never won a state championship.

He was, however, a first team all-league running back his junior and senior year and led his team to the playoffs his senior year. He finished high school with zero discipline incidents and completed two years of Running Start, a dual credit enrollment program; earning his AA degree. He was also nominated for the all-state football game *and broke the school's all-time career rushing record*, a record that was previously set the year he was born. I believe these achievements came because of what Xavier Charles Wicks *believed* he could *become*.

We see these differences in every walk of life. Administrators who spend a career plateaued, and administrators who earn state or national honors. CEOs who maintain steady and predictable results, and CEOs who take the business to the next level, and the next. Entrepreneurs who stumble, sputter and fail, and entrepreneurs who launch businesses out of their garage that change the world. What is the difference? *Being* versus *becoming.*

Every single day, without fail, with students, parents, staff, counselors and anyone else within earshot, I talk about the vision of what we are *becoming* as a high school community. I want them each to remember who they were in the days, weeks, months and years past, and be grateful for the gains they have made personally, professionally, mentally and spiritually. I want them, and I want you, to continue to unleash the potential that still remains. It all begins with what we believe.

At my high school, we believe that we can become the highest performing high school in the state of Washington. Because of that vision, because of what we *believe* we can *become*, we make conscious and deliberate decisions that answer the essential question, "Is this choice helping or holding us back from becoming our best self?" If the choice is holding us back we stop doing it, or we do it differently. If the choice is helping us, we *still* assess how we may be able to do it better to achieve even better results! Thinking differently has us behaving differently which is leading to different results.

Are you content just *being* in the role you are in or are you ready to shift, focus and commit to *becoming* your next best self?

Committing to a morning routine is a great way to initiate and maintain a change process. I have developed my morning routine over the years. At first, it consisted of me getting up with just enough time to shower, get ready and head out the door after kissing my bride goodbye. This was more of a pattern than a routine. I was usually still sleepy, felt rushed, and I was always hungry because I had not given myself enough time to eat. Not only that, I was in kind of a sour mood because I had done nothing to feed my mind or my soul. What a crappy way to start the day! That morning routine was representative of the kind of person I was at the time, but was not representative of or supporting the kind of person I was meant to become.

I wanted to have a joyful, healthy, motivated and inspiring life. And beyond that, I wanted to help others do the same. I remember thinking the best way to do that on a daily basis was to *live* that way. However, my routines and my behavior did not align with my vision. I started by getting up a little earlier, then a little earlier, then earlier still. Each thing I wanted to add to my routine took time. Do you know what I found, though? The more I added to my morning, the more energy I had during the day. I had less fatigue, I was in a better mood and my mind and my soul were right; even though I was getting up, as I mentioned earlier in the book, around 4 a.m. Monday through Friday.

Something special happens that early in the morning. Your brain is wired to be at peak performance at that hour. You know all those times you wake up with a really great idea? You know, the times when you wish you had a pad of paper so you could write it down? Next time that happens, check what time it is.

My morning routine is set up to change me, and keep on changing me. It looks like this:

1. Wake up
2. Get out of bed
3. Get dressed in cycling clothes and sweats
4. Brew the coffee and prep some breakfast
5. Read three devotionals while enjoying breakfast
6. Continue reading, swapping between a couple books
7. Watch YouTube for some motivation or inspiration
8. Ride the Peloton
9. Shower and get ready for work
10. Kiss my bride goodbye

By the time I get to work I have been up for three hours and I feel amazing! I guard and treasure my morning time. My wife notices a difference, my kids notice a difference and my colleagues notice a difference. And most of all, so do I.

You are the sum total of your thoughts and your behaviors. If you want it to start adding up differently, you have to start thinking and behaving differently. We are influenced by the past, and the past influences our future. Yet our experiences right now are constantly becoming our past. We must control the here and now in order to create the future self we want to become. Do not be paralyzed by what *might* happen *if* you change; rather, be propelled by what you *know* will happen *when* you change.

Chapter 16

Taking fear head on

"One of the greatest discoveries a man makes,
one of his great surprises, is to find he can do
what he was afraid he couldn't do." –Henry Ford

In Chapter 7 fear was discussed in regard to why you are standing in your own way. Let's return to the idea and take a deeper dive into fear with the purpose of learning how to get out of your own way.

Want to hear something wild? In 1978, a controversial theory proposed that the world does not exist unless observed and measured. This was unproven until 2015, when a team at Australian National University demonstrated that reality at the quantum level does in fact not exist unless we look at it and measure it. That sounds kind of weird, but it actually makes sense.

Let's apply that theory to the reality of fear. Isn't it true that fear only exists if we choose to see it and give it meaning? I want you to think about which fears you acknowledge in your life, and how much meaning you decide to give them. One of the good habits I have developed over time is reading. Whenever I am writing, no matter what it is–a blog post, an article, a conference proposal or a book–I am also reading. I am energized and inspired by the great works of so many people. As I write this book, I am reading several other amazing books, including *Love Does, Chase the Lion and 5 Marks of a Man.*

Love Does, by Bob Goff, is quickly becoming one of my favorites. When it comes to fear, Bob says this:

"I used to be afraid of failing at the things that mattered to me. Now I am more afraid of succeeding at the things that do not matter."

Man. That seriously resonates with me. Does it resonate with you, too? Bob, you hit the nail on the head with this one (and many others in your book).

In my stage of life, this quote has become my mantra. I wish I had found this wisdom a couple of decades ago. For years I bought into the societal brainwashing that told me I had to dress a certain way, speak a certain way, go to certain places or not go to other places…blah, blah, blah. What a trap.

Looking back, buying into that trap caused me a lot of anxiety.

And while I was afraid of not measuring up to the things I thought mattered, I was also succeeding at the things that do not matter. I got really good at maintaining a certain image; at looking, speaking and acting the part, but I was not doing what I really wanted – helping others become their best self.

We trust a number of tools to steer us in the right direction. Remember when MapQuest was a cutting-edge tool? You could get online on your computer and get step-by-step directions to any destination. You could even print them out and take them with you! Then there was GPS. I remember getting lost on a family trip to the Oregon Coast. What a nightmare. Traveling with our kids on a nine-hour road trip and going in the wrong direction; lost, tired and hungry. It was an unmitigated disaster. When we got back to Spokane, I drove straight to Target and bought a Garmin GPS. Now, most of us use our phone, and with amazing accuracy.

In recorded history, humans have navigated by the sun, moon, stars, and then by compass. The compass works because it points you in the right direction. I like to think of fear as a compass.

Whenever I choose to observe one of my own fears, I study it carefully to see where it is pointing. In this way, I've developed an appreciation for fear. It tends to point out what needs to be done. It's not like the map app on my phone; fear does not tell me every turn to make and when to take it, but it often points me in the right direction. It helps me get to where I'm headed, and better yet, where I need to be going instead.

Thanks to that compass, I feel like I can die a happy man. My marriage is thriving, my kids are happy and healthy, my personal relationship with Jesus is rock solid, *and* (this is very important) in my adult years some very smart and respectable people have told me I remind them of Denzel Washington.

Now *that* is a lifetime achievement! What a compliment to live up to! I have no idea how long I can hold on to that comparison, but I am going to do my best to milk that as long as I can. What I don't understand is what about me reminds these smart and respectable people of Denzel Washington. The reason I am flattered is not just because Denzel is a crazy handsome man. I am flattered because of the view that I have of Denzel's character. I see him as God-fearing, wise, loving, courageous, humble, patient and discerning. These are all definitely qualities I aspire to. Denzel has made it into my morning routine on more than one occasion, and when he does, he never disappoints. Maybe, just maybe, I am a chameleon and I am taking on some of those admirable characteristics by way of watching and listening to him. Mission accomplished!

In 2015, Denzel delivered a commencement speech at the Dillard University graduation ceremony. It was a speech for the ages. There are a number of different uploads of the same speech on YouTube with a total of more than 25 million views. In that speech, he makes three statements that will stick with me forever, and I would like to share them with you.

First, he says ease is a greater corrupter to progress than struggle. How profound is that? Because what do most people do when things get hard? They quit. What do most people do if they even anticipate something will be hard? They give up. It happens every day. I tell my kids all the time that it is not hard to be successful these days–all you have to do is not quit.

There is always a prize at the end of a struggle. It may not necessarily be the pot of gold. It may simply be the fact that you made it through. Either way there is a reward. Either way, you figure out you are more powerful than you ever gave yourself credit.

As an aside, I will say here that quitting is sometimes better for others involved who actually care, because then the quitter does not do any more damage to the team, the job or the project. The greater danger is the person who cuts corners or takes shortcuts; those people end up inflicting more damage.

Denzel's second bit of advice has to do with failing big.

He talks about the big risks he took in his life and career. He talks about why failing big and setting big goals helped him accomplish his big dreams. He points out there were plenty of roles for which he auditioned and did not get selected. He talks about his 1.7 GPA while in college. And he says trying his hardest at the things that mattered, and missing the mark, was better than never trying at all.

I am sharing Denzel's wise words because fear can be the enemy of success. Most of the time, we are afraid of failing. That's why we give up, why we take shortcuts, and why we end up failing small instead of big.

People assume that success and failure are linear; that you try and you either succeed or you do not. The reality is that failure, sometimes multiple failures, are required for ultimate success. Part of taking fear head on is actually seeing the benefit of failing; and sometimes, failing big.

In order to face your fears head on, I need you to get comfortable. No, I don't mean get comfortable as in your pajamas and slippers. I mean get comfortable being uncomfortable. Because that's really at the heart of our fear, isn't it?

Get comfortable with that. I remember talking to the principal of the school where I was first an assistant principal. She had actually been my mentor teacher when I'd started teaching 13 years earlier. I told her that I was settling into the role of school leader because I had finally begun to be comfortable being uncomfortable.

Face it, when you are in leadership of any kind, there are going to be uncomfortable situations. Being able to be at peace with those situations, even when the situations may be challenging, will help you overcome any fear you may have. And as a leader, you will find that peace and overcoming fear are both anchored in loving and caring for others. During his commencement speech, Denzel said one more thing that really resonates with me. He said to put God first. He shared his gratitude for all things and in all things. Denzel gave credit to God for every accomplishment, as well as for the struggles he was fortunate enough to learn from. Denzel says that even though there were times he did not stick with God, God still stuck with him.

I realize that I am writing to believers and non-believers alike; but I'm telling you, if you want to take fear head on, do not do it alone. Denzel may have not explicitly expressed how God's love neutralizes fear; but I can. Knowing I have God's unconditional love, and sharing that love through a life of servant leadership, is what provides me peace in all situations. Remember, we cannot focus on doing good things and stopping bad things at the same time. The same is true for feeling love and feeling fear; we cannot do them at the same time. So I focus on God's love. I do not question, because I know if my focus is on love I am on the right path. As Proverbs 3, 5-6 says, "Trust in the Lord with all your heart and lean not on your own understanding. In all your ways submit to him and he will make your paths straight."

I recently heard Will Smith tell a great story about fear. He was taking a break for a couple days from a film he was making. He and some friends were having dinner and drinks when someone called out, "Hey, let's go skydiving tomorrow!"

Everyone in the group erupted with shouts and cheering, all in agreement that skydiving was a great idea. Even Will cheered, although he describes his cheering as a bit of a mask for the fear he immediately felt when he imagined jumping from a plane at 14,000 feet. I would be scared as could be, too.

If you've read or listened to anything from Will Smith, you know he has an obsessive love-hate relationship with fear. In this particular story, Will talks about not being able to sleep that night. He would doze off, then wake up suddenly with fears of skydiving. It irritated him that this was happening, especially while he was safe in his bed. Because at that point in time, there was nothing to be afraid of. The next morning, he could barely even eat or drink. On the way to the airfield, in the van with his friends, the atmosphere was upbeat and Will wondered if anyone else was faking it besides him.

Before he knew it, he was up in the plane, sitting on the instructor's lap (which is a really funny part of the story) making small talk. Will says when you jump for the first time you are attached to an instructor who guides the jump. The attachment also helps get you out of the plane. The instructors say they are going to count to three, but they only count to two, because on three the rookie jumpers always grab the sides of the open door.

So, on two, Will and his instructor were freefalling. Will says that for the first seconds he felt sheer terror. Absolute and utter terror. Then, Will says something interesting happened. First, he says it didn't feel like he was falling; he actually felt like he was flying. Then, he says, his terror turned into the most blissful feeling he has ever had. Will concludes his story with this:

"At that moment you realize you have zero fear. You realize that at the point of maximum danger is the point of minimum fear; and it is *bliss*. God placed the best things in life on the other side of fear."

Will Smith says *he* has daily confrontations with fear. Will Smith! One of the most confident and successful Hollywood personalities. *He* has daily confrontations with fear? Wow. That really puts it into perspective, right? Will readies himself for fear so it does not have power over him. Then, he takes it head on.

By now you know about my best fitness investment to date; my Peloton bike. I love my Peloton. I'm not one of the crazy fanatics, but I did put in some time in 2019. Here are those stats:

- 8,185 total minutes
- Average 175 watts per ride
- Average 20 mph per ride
- 2,716 total miles
- 114,417 total calories burned

I am proud of those stats because they represent a lot more than just the numbers. There is always a story behind the data. I have a number of inspirational stories from my time on the Peloton. All the instructors are fantastic, but one instructor who has grown on me is professional cyclist and gold medal winner Christine D'Ercole. Christine has an amazing story of finding cycling and finding herself. She tells it way better than I do, but essentially she found cycling by way of an identity crisis.

Christine is not built like a cover model. She is the first to tell you that. In my opinion, looking like a cover model, for a man or woman, should not be something you have to come to grips with. It should just be. Same, in reverse, for the cover model not feeling a complex because they are not built like a gold medal cyclist.

Christine has the body of a track cyclist. She is built for power and it is awesome. On a recent Peloton ride with Christine as the instructor, she said something that really struck me. I will say that the extra blood flow to the brain during exercise is pretty amazing for having epiphanies! The bike is where I go to struggle and find myself. For me, riding the Peloton is a metaphor for the triumphs and the spoils of life.

To tell the story about Christina, I will need to say *Sorry Pearl!* in advance. It was December 26, 2019, the day after Christmas. We were 14 minutes and 50 seconds into the ride, and we had just kicked up the resistance to a difficult level. Christine asked the class a question. If we had to, did we think we could handle the rest of the ride for the next 45 minutes at that resistance? It seemed impossible. But then she said this:

"Yes, you could. Do you know how? You *calm the f*ck down*. You breathe...and you remember why you ride, you remember what you want, but most importantly you remember that *you are worth it*...you are worth this fight."

And that is life's struggles, in a nutshell.

Here you are, already gasping for air at 15 minutes of a 45 minute ride. You are afraid to finish. You are contemplating whether or not you should just quit the ride.

I had a head cold. My body ached, I couldn't breathe and I definitely wanted to quit. Want to know what I did? I thought about the people I needed to be strong for. I thought, if I am going to be strong for them when they need me in the future, I need to build the foundation now. So I calmed the f*ck down, I breathed and I remembered the fight was worth it.

I finished that ride, and so, my friend, will you.

Words to Remember

1. Thinking shapes behavior, page 117
2. Finish your medicine, page 132
3. If you want to change your personal reality, change your personality, page 138
4. Do good things, page 144
5. Inspiration is all around use, page 154

Call to Action

You have just finished Part III. These chapters have been an explicit call to action, a guide to doing the work necessary to get out of your own way. Next, we will learn how great life really can be when you are out of your own way, once and for all. Please get out your paper and pen once again. Here are the questions to answer before we move forward:

1. Thinking shapes behavior. How has your thinking created the conditions you are in right now? How will your *thinking* need to change for *you* to change?
2. If you were to complete a chart like the one in Chapter 12, what problems would you see? What potential solutions might you try?
3. Do a little research of your own on the Map of Consciousness, quantum physics and the Reticular Activating System. This is complex and exciting stuff.

Hopefully, like me, you come away with more questions than answers!

4. Are your windows dirty? Do you know other people who have dirty windows? What do you need to do to clean up your own windows? What light has been blocked in and out while your windows were dirty?

5. What is the hardest part of change for you?

6. Have you ever experienced a moment like Will Smith when he jumped out of that airplane? That moment when you realized the bliss waiting for you on the other side of fear?

NOTES:

Part IV: *What* will change when you get out of the way?

Chapter 17

Everything will change

"You can't go back and change the beginning, but you can start where you are and change the ending." –C.S. Lewis

Once you get out of your own way, everything will be different; forever.

Yes, I know that's a bold statement, but it's true. And notice I didn't say everything would always be *better*. You will still experience loss, heartache, disappointment and every other hardship that comes with being human. In fact, you might experience some of the same hardships you did while you were still standing in your own way.

The difference is this: you will not have *yourself* to overcome any longer. That is one thing you can count on and one less thing to battle. It's a very good thing when you can count on yourself.

You already know the story of how I got out of my own way. It has been quite a journey, and continues to be. I am a living, breathing testament that anyone can get out of their own way. Really. If I can do it, you can do it, too.

Yes, everything will be different when you get out of your own way, but please understand, it takes time. I did not get out of my own way overnight. It was not like passing through a magic portal, and on the other side I was a new man. Instead, it was a long, hard and rewarding grind.

I had to earn it. I still do. I put in the hours each day. And that is what makes it one of life's greatest achievements. Most people are their own worst enemy. Sometimes in life it's a lot easier to find your adversaries than it is to find your allies. The same is true when you are searching yourself for help. Your worst self is going to be way too easy to find. It will jump right up and volunteer. Instead, look for the quiet kid in the back row. That's your winning teammate. That's your best self, ready to help you save the day.

Sticking with this lifelong project will take commitment, support and all the right tools. There may be hurdles you can't even imagine yet. And that is why this process also takes faith.

By nature, I like things to be a certain way. I work well with teams, but I enjoy working alone, too. That way I know what is coming around the corner. When I get home, I always hang up the car keys in the same place so I know where they are when it's time to drive again. I like order and I like things in their place. So you will be amused to know that when I walk into my family kitchen and I count nine cupboard doors open for no good reason, it blows my mind. The name for my thinking style is concrete sequential. And the need for predictability is a common characteristic for a mind like mine.

The difference is that I have a strong Christian faith. Faith flies in the face of predictability. Faith is a belief in something you cannot yet touch or see. And that is what you need to step boldly forward into becoming your very best self.

The amazing thing about God is that He does not keep us guessing. He affirms that faith, albeit in His own perfect time, by revealing his love for us when He answers prayer. And He knows what is best for us without us even asking.

Have faith. Know that everything will be better when you get out of your own way. As you make progress, you will be affirmed. Believe in that, and you will always continue to make progress on your journey.

Here's an undeniable truth: When one thing changes, another changes. Sometimes in unforeseen ways. It applies just about everywhere. If your tire goes flat and you keep driving around, your steering is going to be affected, too, as well as your speed. If you do your best to eat clean for several weeks, you will probably lose some weight, maybe start to sleep better and just feel better in general, too.

Life is full of these chain reactions; some predictable, some not. But there is one thing I can predict with 100 percent certainty, if you begin changing major aspects of your life, other areas will follow.

It's a lot like the relationship between the sides of a triangle. The three sides are interdependent and rely on one another to keep the triangle's shape. Take one side away and it is no longer a triangle. And if one of the sides changes, all the sides change.

Our lives are like that. If one major aspect of us changes, the other major aspects of us will change, too. This may work in our favor or it may work against us. But when you are working on becoming your best self, if you hone in on one area, your whole self is going to increase as well.

Jim Rohn is a respected entrepreneur, author and motivational speaker. His message is clear-cut and it resonates with me. Here's an example:

"If you want life to change, you have to change. If you want life to get better, you have to get better."

I love that. In my morning routine, and throughout my day, I have learned to focus on certain virtues, values and characteristics. These are designed, not only to make me better, but to contribute to the betterment of those around me. And they work!

To me, this means everything. When I tell you it will all be different when you get out of your own way, this is exactly what I'm talking about.

One of my favorite chapters in the Bible is Corinthians 13. It describes the way of love with beautiful words like these:

"And if I have prophetic powers, and understand all mysteries and all knowledge, and if I have all faith, so as to remove mountains, but have not love, I am nothing….Love is patient and kind; love does not envy or boast; it is not arrogant… Faith, hope, and love. But the greatest of these is love."

These are words to live by my friends. But as long as you are standing in your own way, these words will fall on deaf ears. What can you expect to be different when you get out of the way? Love.

What else can you expect to feel when you get out of the way? Peace.

It's hard to find the words to describe the internal struggle that occurs when you are living a life that is you against you. If you are living that life right now, you know exactly what I'm talking about. I can tell you this, though. When I did the work, and I allowed my best self to come forward, there is one word that best describes how I felt when I lay my head on the pillow at night. And that word is peace.

What else can you expect when you get out of the way? Joy.

Sometimes we confuse joy with happiness. But happiness can be fleeting. Even when you are miserable, you can find something to bring you moments of happiness. An ice cream cone might make you temporarily happy. So might your new 60" TV. If you are miserable, seeing other people be miserable can make you happy, for crying out loud! But none of those things can bring joy. Happiness is dependent on external factors, while joy comes from within. True joy doesn't happen until you are your best self. Joy takes inner peace. Joy means satisfaction in sacrificing for others.

Want another wonderful benefit of getting out of the way? It is wisdom.

If we go way back in history, the richest man to ever live was not Jeff Bezos. He is worth a mere $193 billion as I write this. It's not Mansa Musa, either. Mansa, ruler of the Mali Empire in the 13th century, was worth an estimated $400 billion in his day. No, the man I speak of is King Solomon, King of Israel, worth over $2 trillion at his peak. Yet King Solomon, a very religious king, never prayed for wealth. Instead, he prayed for wisdom which, according to history, God provided in abundance. This wisdom allowed King Solomon to make some very profitable decisions.

Getting out of the way will give you another marvelous quality: discernment.

When you are in your own way, you tend to make selfish decisions. Of course you do! You're looking out for number one. You are likely not considering others much at all. You may be decisive when you are in your own way, but you are not discerning. What's the difference? Decisive means to make a definitive decision. Once that decision is made, it is made. That can be okay sometimes. But it will never beat discernment, which is the ability to judge *well*. And here goes what sounds like a tongue-twister, but is very true: A well-discerned decision can be decisive, but decisiveness without discernment is destructive.

What else can you expect to be different when you get out of the way? Most definitely courage.

It's tough to be courageous when you are standing in the way, always casting the long shadow of doubt. When someone gets in the way, that's what they do. They cast doubt. The last thing someone in the way wants is someone with courage. When I finally got out of my own way, I could see the difference in my own eyes, and I liked what I saw. The new courageous me spoke up in meetings, when before, I'd stayed silent. The new me offered my ideas, when before, I'd always been afraid my ideas weren't good enough. When I got out of my own way I wrote and published this book; but if I had stayed in my own way I would have taken that unwritten book to the grave.

When you get out of the way, you will find strength.

I've always had a certain mental toughness, grit, steadfastness; that whatever-it-takes kind of strength. But when I was in my own way I would have to fight with myself to be strong. I had to fight to not quit. When I got out of my own way there was no longer a fight. Instead of an adversary, I now have an ally, and quitting is not an option.

When you get out of the way you will find patience.

I believe patience is a combination of virtues including love, peace, wisdom, and discernment. And maybe the courage to be vulnerable, too. Unlike my natural tendency toward strength, patience has not always been a virtue for me. When I was in my own way I was lacking in all those virtues, so it is no wonder that my patience was so deficient. I have a lot of regret looking back on my lack of patience. That's where this chapter's quote resonates so strongly with me. "You can start where you are and change the ending." What a gift.

When you are out of the way you will find gratitude.

Picture yourself in your own way, grinding out yet another difficult day. You wake up when it's dark to go to work, and by the time you get home it's already dark again. I'm guessing that gratitude is the last thing on your mind. For years, I was annoyed with every bit of that grind, when instead, I should have been ecstatic that I had a secure job to provide for my family. Like every one of the other virtues I'm sharing with you, gratitude is a choice. The problem is, when you are in your own way it is like one of those telephone scramblers used to disguise conversations in World War II. When you are in your own way, your priorities are all scrambled up and you don't realize how much you have to be thankful for. Recognizing gratitude is now part of my morning routine. I can't, and I won't, go a day without it.

And here is one more wonderful quality that will be yours when you are out of the way. Grace.

It's a magical thing. The extension of kindness to the undeserving with no expectation of anything in return. In today's society, it just does not make any sense. Why would someone do something for someone else? Especially when they don't deserve it? Without reward or recognition? That's absurd! No, it's magic. It's just what you start to do when you are no longer in your own way. Most people go around thinking their personal, professional and spiritual life is just happening to them. But nothing in life just *happens*. Most people underestimate or, worse yet, totally neglect, how much influence they have on any given situation, including their own development and evolution. Don't let that happen to you!

Imagine climbing a spiral staircase, or hiking an upward trail, toward a beautiful scenic view. I have done this dozens of times, maybe you have, too. As you gain elevation, through the window or through the clearing, the view is that much sweeter, clearer, and vast. Each is the perfect metaphor for the recurring transformation that occurs when people apply knowledge to themselves over time. Every time you apply all this good stuff you reach the next level. Then it's time to keep going, up and around once more. I cannot tell you how many times I ventured out, in pursuit of a magnificent scenic view, before I realized the alignment to the metaphor for life. Do the work, move a little higher. Reach the next level, see a little more clearly. Stay the course, build a little more stamina. Make it to the top, look for the next peak to crest!

Stay out of your own way, keep doing what you know is right for yourself and for others, and I promise you that life will never, ever be the same again.

Chapter 18

The Gift of Opportunity

"A pessimist sees the difficulty in every opportunity; an optimist sees the opportunity in every difficulty." –Winston S. Churchill

Well, you've nearly made it through this book. I am grateful you did!

Did you find only difficulty in these pages? Perhaps you said to yourself, *That sounds like a lot of work. I'll never be able to do all that.*

I'm hoping instead that you found opportunity.

As you know by now, that opportunity is found in the difficulty. Yes, I expect it to be hard. I expect this book to challenge you, stretch you and hammer you. But I also expect it to be rewarding beyond measure. I expect it to help build you into the best you could possibly be.

Funny, isn't it? That based on your attitude and approach, this book could either discourage or encourage you? I'll be honest, I've read these pages dozens of times now. Even though I lived this story myself and know every bit of it by heart, I still find opportunity in these words every time I read them. I hope that meaning is clear for you, too.

When you get out of your own way, opportunity is everywhere.

Your ears hear differently now. Your nose smells differently now. Your mouth speaks differently now. Your hands, feet, legs and mind all work differently now. Your eyes see differently now. Things that did not even register as an opportunity before will register now. Thomas Edison said this:

"Most people miss opportunity because it is dressed in overalls and looks like work."

Isn't it amazing? Your eyes will see the opportunity under the overalls, and the rest of your best self will be chomping at the bit to do the work. Not only will opportunities look different, but you will also attract different and better opportunities. You see, it's all connected. You are where you are because of who you are. When you are different, you will end up in different places, and those different places will hold different opportunities.

By changing your personality, you have changed your personal reality. People will begin to see you as an asset. Opportunities tend to benefit others, too. When others see you as an asset, bigger and better opportunities come your way.

Here is another nugget of wisdom from author Bob Goff:

"We don't need more opportunities, we need a better attitude."

I pray for this kind of wisdom. While we know more opportunities will come our way when our best self is in the driver's seat, Bob is suggesting that the opportunities are already here. When we change our attitude, when we change ourselves, then those opportunities are abundant. Our hearts and minds are ready to embrace those opportunities to the utmost.

Once you get past you, the doors are open. When you get past you, you are achieving your own full potential. But most exciting and important of all, when you get past you, you are helping others reach their full potential.

I want you to highlight that last sentence. I want you to burn it into your brain. This is life's ultimate purpose.

In the movie *Pay It Forward*, a student played by Haley Joel Osment has a simple idea that he believes can change the world. He starts out by trying to help his single mom; played by Helen Hunt. Along the way, the idea of paying it forward becomes a national phenomenon. After the movie came out, life mirrored art as people around the world made a point of paying acts of kindness forward to other people.

The movie is based on a novel of the same name by Catherine Ryan Hyde, but the phrase originated in the 1912 book *In the Garden of Delight* by Lily Hardy Hammond, where she says, "You don't pay love back, you pay it forward."

How fitting is it that the phrase originated as not just an act of kindness, but an act of unselfish love? You getting out of your own way is an act of love. It is an act of you loving yourself enough to stand down and step up. Now that your best self has emerged, it is time to pay it forward.

It all comes down to purpose. On its first pages, this book promised to tell the truth about revealing your purpose. And in these final pages, we find that accepting the truth and doing something with that truth brings life's greatest reward: knowing your purpose.

Having purpose gives life incredible meaning. Your purpose is unique. Your purpose shines a light on your gifts. Once you find your purpose, it is yours to develop and to share. It could be big or small. It does not matter whether it matters to someone else. Whether your purpose is cutting hair or splitting neutrons, it becomes profound by the nature of your commitment to it.

I am not the first expert on becoming your best self. I will not be the last. Someone reading this book has dreamed of doing what I am doing and is going to put this book down and go write their own. The goal–and the reward–of getting out of your own way is ultimately to help others do the same.

I want to leave you with this closing thought from Les Brown:

"A dog can't be anything but a dog, a tree can't be anything but a tree. YOU have unlimited potential. You can put effort on you, and by concentrating on you and developing you, you can transform your life no matter where you are right now."

We are the only living creatures that get to choose. Choose you, and choose to get out of your own way.

Words to Remember (throughout the entire book)

1. Wisdom
2. Love
3. Strength
4. Courage
5. Patience
6. Discernment
7. Gratitude
8. Grace
9. Peace
10. Joy

Call to Action

Congratulations! You have just finished Part IV, What will be different when you get out of your own way? It's a journey to get through this book. You have taken fear head on, you have faced your childhood trauma and you have come to grips that it was you all along who stood in the way of you becoming everything you are meant to be. I can't wait to see what you are going to accomplish! Here are some questions to ponder:

1. I shared with you how different everything was when I got out of my own way. What is your everything? What can you envision being different when you are out of your own way? What do you need to help you? Who do you need to help you?

2. How is paying it forward part of you becoming your best self? What does that look like? What chain reaction can you start?

3. Many people overlook the importance of having a personal vision. Do you have a vision for the person you want to become? Have you shared that with anyone? How does your vision of yourself benefit others? What habits and routines need to be in place for you to cultivate that vision?

Final Call to Action

Being shown and taught how to get out of your own way, then doing it, is a massive achievement. You should be proud of that. However, ultimate fulfillment is achieved by giving the gift of helping someone else get out of their own way. The final call to action is lending this book to someone you care about, then, walking alongside them as they realize the answers to the question, what is standing in the way?

Share your story with me and others you think may benefit. Share the story of your own journey as it unfolds, at **www.whatisstandingintheway.me**.

NOTES:

Preview Andre's next book, *Motivate Me*, and leave your feedback at *www.becomingmybestself.net*.

MOTIVATE ME:

A Guide to Motivating Those You Lead

"Do the best you can until you know better. Then when you know better, do better." –Maya Angelou

4 a.m. comes early, every time. I reach over and silence my alarm, and I pause a few breaths to let myself fully wake up before I climb out of bed. Even on the days of the year with 12+ hours of daylight, it is still dark at 4 a.m. I like it. It's quiet. It's peaceful. It's time to begin my beloved morning routine of continuous improvement.

What if I told you that improving yourself was ridiculously easy? Got your attention? Good! When I tell you the secret, you will indeed be amazed.

Actually, when I tell you the secret you will more likely slap your palm to your forehead and say, "Duh!" I know this because I figuratively, and sometimes literally, slap my palm to my forehead, dismayed that people who are responsible for getting results either don't understand this simple principle or aren't disciplined enough to follow it.

Are you ready? The secret to improvement is...to *focus* on improvement.

Wait a minute! What?

I know what you're thinking. *Andre has lost it. With a ridiculous statement like that, he will never work again as an author, a coach, or a consultant.*

But read on and you will understand why what I'm saying is absolutely true. Many organizations, businesses, teams, and individuals focus only on results or outcomes. They say things like, "Our goal is to win a state championship" or "Our goal is to convert 75% of our cold calls to actual sales" or "our goal is a 95% graduation rate." Whatever your industry, I will bet you have been part of these conversations. These goals are often inspiring, but what goes wrong? Why are these impressive goals consistently unmet?

I'll tell you why. There is a marked difference between wanting to improve, hoping to improve, pretending you improved... and actually focusing on improvement. Focusing on improvement has one prerequisite that wanting, hoping and pretending do not. And that is commitment.

Leaders, for your own growth and for the growth of those you lead, make sure you are always focused on improvement. And if your organization, business, team, students, or client truly wants to focus on improvement, they must commit to two key factors: development and evaluation. Understand the importance of documenting and rewarding improvement. Do not focus on wins; instead, focus on the factors that lead to wins. It begins and ends with a focus on and commitment to continuous improvement.

The opposite of improvement is apathy, complacency, fatigue or burnout (when caused by a lack of self care), romanticising about the way things used to be, and/or lack of leadership ability. These all contribute to the curse of the steady downward slide to mediocrity. Without a clear and consistently communicated priority on improvement, things fail to improve or may even get worse.

If you are a leader of any kind you can benefit from measuring improvement. And aren't we all leaders to those around us? But especially you CEOs, directors, managers, coaches, teachers and principals. Determine what metrics can be measured recurrently to see if your people (or you) are improving. What skills and abilities, if developed, documented, displayed, recognized and rewarded will have a direct correlation to improvement?

We know this works in education. Teachers and principals across the world use frameworks of best practices to identify and evaluate areas of improvement. When this is done with fidelity, teachers improve, student learning improves and graduation rates improve. Notice the focus is not on the end result, although long-term vision *is* important in setting up the framework. The focus should always be on improvement. And because of that, the purpose of evaluation is to provide feedback that will support further development.

Athletic coaches may measure the 40-yard dash, the squat and the bench press. Sales managers may measure sales conversion, quote to close or return customers. Non-profit organizations may measure the impact of clients served. Regardless of your industry there are metrics that correlate success and those metrics can be evaluated and developed.

The secondary purpose of evaluation is to archive and compare improvement. Most industries have standards. So what happens if the standard is met early and often? Or met but never improved? What happens if there is no incentive to continue growing? I will tell you what happens; over time, apathy and complacency happen and the organization suffers.

The priority of improvement can be made crystal clear when incentives and rewards are tied to improvement; bonuses, rewards, accolades, advancement, promotions, playing time. These examples should not necessarily be predicated on improvement, however, improvement must be a factor for each of these decisions.

So why is improvement so evasive? Because it takes more time and effort than not improving. Because sometimes the return on investment is nominal. Because it takes courage. Because it takes a sustained effort. Because it takes sacrifice. Because sometimes you have to suffer. It might be uncomfortable. Let's face it, improvement is evasive because it is usually hard to improve. Improvement can also be evasive if the focus and commitment are weak.

Many organizations actually have structures for development of all kinds: professional development, physical, spiritual and relational. However, these structures are often unstructured; meaning there is no connection between the opportunity for development and the poorly communicated or uncommunicated priority of improvement. Athletes will often avoid the weight room unless they know their strength and speed are a requisite to move up on the depth chart. Employees will take advantage of the free professional library when they know the direct benefit of their knowledge and application of knowledge is promotion.

An incredibly powerful transformation happens when people know what they need to do to improve and that improvement is associated with incentives and tied to reaching goals.

With any individual, group, team, or organization I have ever led, one of the most significant challenges to a commitment to continuous improvement is what to do when it gets uncomfortable. In my experience, most people find being transparent with their own "stuff" is the biggest challenge. People don't want to talk about that. They don't really want to talk about the troubled past that has them standing in their own way. People do not want to talk about the reason why overall sales are down in their department. People do not want to really talk about why students are transferring out of their school to another school. What do you do when faced with this challenge? Individuals, groups, teams, and organizations that are truly committed to continuous improvement take that fear head on. Your best self is depending on it!

Your story is predicated on your ability to focus on continuous improvement. Imagine you have committed 3-5 years, maybe more, to leading your business, your school, or your organization -- to turn the curve, to increase sales, improve graduation rate, reduce waste; whatever measuring stick you use to indicate success or growth. Do any of these scenarios resonate with you? At the end of your term, there *is* going to be a story to tell. So the question begs, who is telling your story, and what will it say about you?

Leaders, I want to call your attention to something; you are not only a leader, you are an author. Are you going to take the "pen" and write the narrative of that story?

In literature, there are characters that play roles and give a story life; they take a story down this path or that path, around twists and turns, and the story eventually leads up to a crescendo...or sometimes to tragedy. The author controls that and narrates the details that give the characters and the story meaning.

I vividly recall one morning in 2011. I was driving to work thinking about my task list for the day. I got to work, began on my list and when the day was done I got in my car to drive home and I thought to myself, "Where is all this going? What is it leading to? And who is making it happen?" I had been a teacher, coach, or administrator for 15 years at that point. I felt like I was doing good work; I was living inspired and others had told me I inspired them. But, it felt like things were just happening; my story was sort of writing itself. In fact, there was more to the story than met the eye; and I was not exactly playing the role I was intended to play.

I realized that we all have the opportunity to write the narrative of the story we want to tell and the story to <u>be told</u> after we are done writing it. I realized that every few days was a new page, every few weeks a new chapter, every couple years a new book in the series. I realized that I was surrounded by the characters in my story; that I was an architect with influence to shape the characters' role and whether or not new characters were to make their way into the story.

I put this thinking to the test when I launched THEZONE Project, a community-wide collective impact initiative that harnessed the collective prowess of neighbors and other community leaders across all sectors to accomplish one shared vision: Improve the environment where our children and families live as a means of increasing the graduation rate. Seizing the moment(s) of authoring this story required me to do a few things that each of us, as leaders and authors, must do:

- **Have a vision.** Nothing is more important as an author than being able to "write" with the end in mind. Having a vision will anchor every leadership decision you make;
- **Share the vision.** A story with one character is a boring story. Even the Old Man in the Sea had a fish in his story! Colleagues, employees, stakeholders, family, friends are

all part of the story. Help them to see and commit to the end you have in mind;

- **Make the vision mutually beneficial.** We are all part of a number of different stories. Help others see the reciprocal benefit of playing a role in your story. Better yet, let them feel like the story is one of their own;

- **Cultivate the vision.** Have you ever noticed how characters develop over the course of a story? Has it ever dawned on you the author makes that happen? Leaders, we play a significant role in "character development." Clarify your characters' purpose, provide autonomy to self-develop, and allow for mastery of that development.

With the changing tides of the latest and greatest takes on leadership fundamentals, we need some fundamentals that are enduring. Tides come in, and tides go out. Morning, midday, evening; one thing is irrefutable. It is just water. There are endless books, videos, articles - and blogs - with tips, tricks, and suggestions for becoming and staying a great leader. Those are important, but there has to be a foundation from which you operate. For me it is this…

Your staff, your employees, any stakeholders, and especially you are characters in the story you are crafting as a leader and author. Give life and give meaning to each character. Do not fall victim to allowing a story to just write itself and letting it just end any which way. Decide right now how you want the story to end and begin "writing" the narrative, chapter by chapter of the paths, twists, and turns that lead to your vision of an amazing crescendo!

I love the parallels between a story and a life lived. As the story develops, so do you. A savvy author sees the end before he or she even begins writing. Then, the author spends the rest of the story developing the characters into whatever they need to become to fulfill the story's destiny. That is the power you have as the author of *your* story!

◆——————————————————————◆

Andre's new book, *MOTIVATE ME: A Guide to Motivating Those You Lead*, will be available in the Spring of 2022. Follow Andre on LinkedIn to stay connected with his work and to get sneak peeks into his latest work.

Visit **www.whatisstandingintheway.me** and **www.becomingmybestself.net** to share your stories and to read the stories of others who are focused on continuous improvement, getting out of their own way, and becoming their best self.

Notes

Part I

- https://www.cottercrunch.com/ways-you-might-be-standing-in-your-way-to-success/
- https://www.solutionstoallyourproblems.com/5-ways-you-might-be-standing-in-the-way-of-your-best-life/
- https://www.joedibianca.com/whats-standing-in-your-way
- https://www.huffpost.com/entry/success-and-motivation_b_5000797/amp
- https://www.lifecoachcode.com/2017/05/07/signs-you-are-your-own-worst-enemy/
- https://www.huffpost.com/entry/signs-that-you-are-your-own-worst-enemy_n_59e6499ce4b08f9f9edb1cc3?guccounter=1&guce_r eferrer=aHR0cHM6Ly93d3cuZ29vZ2xlLmNvbS8&guce_refe rrer_sig=AQAAAMUyLJSS4QqIq9QUN9fXRPGEwDFvXX7 pJAuVnrPP9x-dHhI5vH4e8fXrEGV0AegsciSonqTCk4Bzb58zGhuNSRwI9V tqZ2C2hMh1VZIMoo6xl3AOEa6OHt3TWTvblZbERmI9f5m ZF-USbQZzZiT4KxqvBbiVRYDaQrsK5IGjBZNI
- https://www.psychologytoday.com/us/blog/stretching-theory/201809/how-many-decisions-do-we-make-each-day
- https://jessicahartung.com/2019/02/27/peers-in-decision-making/
- Winning Decisions. Get it Right the First Time, Schoemaker and Russo
- https://www.huffingtonpost.ca/natasha-koifman/define-personal-brand-advice_b_8220352.html
- https://www.ted.com/talks/lizzie_velasquez_how_do_you_defi ne_yourself?language=en
- http://www.culturequest.us/aboriginal_tools/boomerang.htm
- https://www.businessinsider.com/americans-name-the-top-10-historic-events-that-shaped-their-lifetimes-2016-12#2-president-barack-obamas-election-10

Notes

Part II

- https://www.youtube.com/watch?v=2RuCfTiCDjs&list=WL&index=28&t=0s
- https://www.youtube.com/watch?v=1XDpa2HLXV0&list=WL&index=5
- https://www.cdc.gov/violenceprevention/childabuseandneglect/acestudy/aboutace.html
- https://www.inlander.com/spokane/understanding-aces/Content?oid=2386137
- https://www.npr.org/sections/health-shots/2015/03/02/387007941/take-the-ace-quiz-and-learn-what-it-does-and-doesnt-mean
- https://www.psychologytoday.com/us/blog/the-last-best-cure/201508/8-ways-people-recover-post-childhood-adversity-syndrome
- Fostering Resilient Learners, Pete Hall and Kristen Souers, ASCD 2017
- https://www.briantracy.com/blog/personal-success/fight-or-flight-overcoming-your-fears/
- https://www.cnn.com/2015/10/29/health/science-of-fear/index.html
- https://www.smithsonianmag.com/science-nature/what-happens-brain-feel-fear-180966992/
- https://www.psychologytoday.com/us/blog/hide-and-seek/201205/our-hierarchy-needs

Notes

Part III

- https://study.com/academy/lesson/reticular-activating-system-definition-function.html
- https://medium.com/desk-of-van-schneider/if-you-want-it-you-might-get-it-the-reticular-activating-system-explained-761b6ac14e53
- http://www.psychologydiscussion.net/brain/functions-of-reticular-activating-system-ras-brain-neurology/2893
- https://www.youtube.com/watch?v=2iPFtZENEq4
- https://www.livescience.com/33816-quantum-mechanics-explanation.html
- https://markahaughtonquantumvibrationalnumbers.com/quantum-mechanics-of-the-law-of-attraction/
- https://www.youtube.com/watch?v=bLyqJdz3-Hg
- https://www.forbes.com/sites/chadorzel/2015/07/08/six-things-everyone-should-know-about-quantum-physics/#6d6526bc7d46
- https://www.youtube.com/watch?v=2RuCfTiCDjs&t=709s
- https://www.youtube.com/watch?v=2iPFtZENEq4&t=421s
- https://youtu.be/XEiYKJGiLtl
- https://www.today.com/popculture/can-anyone-really-heal-bad-childhood-wbna10695668
- https://phys.org/news/2015-05-quantum-theory-weirdness.html
- https://www.sciencealert.com/reality-doesn-t-exist-until-we-measure-it-quantum-experiment-confirms
- https://www.forbes.com/sites/quora/2017/09/25/would-the-universe-still-exist-if-no-life-existed-to-observe-it/#54c6f346bbcb
- https://www.youtube.com/watch?v=Hpd61o6TvXM

Notes

Part IV

- https://archive.org/details/InTheGardenOfDelight/page/n221
- Love Does, Bob Goff
- https://www.biblegateway.com/passage/?search=1+Corinthians+13%3A13&version=NIV
- https://www.psychologies.co.uk/joy-vs-happiness
- https://www.psychologies.co.uk/joy-vs-happiness
- https://www.cnbc.com/2018/07/16/jeff-bezos-is-now-the-richest-man-in-modern-history.html
- https://www.bbc.com/news/world-africa-47379458

Author Bio

Andre, his wife Michelle and their four children—Isaac, Xavier, Olivia and Pearl—live in Spokane, Washington. Andre is an impassioned K- 12 veteran educator who, from 2013-2017, leveraged his adaptive leadership ability to begin collaboratively and holistically transforming one of the most distressed areas of Washington State.

Andre is a graduate of Whitworth University in Spokane and earned a master's degree from Lesley University in Cambridge, MA. His work has been published in *Washington Educator Magazine*, *The Inlander* and the *Spokesman Review*. He was presented the John Kohls Excellence in Leadership Award in 2015 and was named a Washington State Regional Assistant Principal of the Year in 2014.

He has an unyielding desire to serve others, a characteristic he has put to use over the past two decades in his career as an award-winning school administrator, teacher, athletic coach and community advocate.

Andre has served on the Spokane Mayor's Advisory Council on Multicultural Affairs, the Spokane Regional Law and Justice Council and the Mayor's Housing Quality and Affordability Task Force. Most notably, he spent nearly four years as the Director of THEZONE project, a place-based collective impact initiative focused on bringing a holistic and comprehensive approach to community revitalization to the neighborhoods of northeast Spokane.

Andre is an entrepreneur, keynote speaker, and motivational speaker across age levels and across sectors. He consults, presents and provides professional development to non-profit organizations, K-12 education, higher education and businesses across the country. He addresses individual clients, small teams and large auditoriums with equal authenticity, integrity, and humility. As a servant leader, he relishes in helping others reach their potential.

Made in the USA
Las Vegas, NV
17 April 2021